THE ULTIMATE MONEY SKILLS HANDBOOK FOR TEENS

A SIMPLIFIED GUIDE TO EARNING, BUDGETING, SAVING, INVESTING, AND CREATING A POSITIVE MONEY MINDSET FOR LIFETIME SUCCESS AND FINANCIAL INDEPENDENCE

C. K. ROY

TABLE OF CONTENTS

INTRODUCTION

If I were to tell you that you're about ten years ahead of most people in learning the value of money just by reading this book, would you believe me? It's true! I didn't realize how important it was and didn't really start understanding until I was already out of college. I got my first job as a caddy when I was 12 and had part-time and summer jobs throughout school. I paid my bills but spent all the rest on having fun and traveling. I graduated with no car, $8000 in student loans and not a penny saved. How I wish I had this book to guide me from that first job! You're in luck though, you have it. So, let's get to learning, shall we?

Looking at statistical patterns, we can spot trends and predict future behaviors—like having our own fortune teller's crystal ball. For example, stats tell us which artist has the most listeners, what's trending in the market, what videos just went viral, and who has the highest scoring average among our favorite sports players. In terms of finances, stats are great because they let us know exactly which path we're on regarding our financial health. But what does this have to do with gaining *The Ultimate Money Skills*?

Well, we need to turn to stats to understand what we're working with regarding our money and the future money we can make. Statistics show that the average American teen makes between $2,000 and $3,000 per month from part-time jobs and their allowance combined. Some teens may not have a part-time job yet and only have access to an allowance. In the future, when these teens begin working, they too will earn around what the stats predict.

These same stats show that everyday teens save about 2% of their earnings. That works out to between $480 to $720 saved per year for most teens. Not too shabby. Of course, that's just an estimate— some teens rake in way more bank from sweet gigs and numerous b-day checks and cash. But most are probably stashing away a few hundred bucks a year. Those stats look pretty good—right?

Not to be a downer, but there's another statistic we need to know: only 22% of teens actually know how to grow their money by investing and the magic of compound interest. Ouch! So, teens have much room for improvement when handling their hard-earned cash! Before we collectively freak out, there's hope on the horizon, so sit tight for a moment—we'll get to the good stuff soon! For now, we must know what we can achieve when we have the right money-savvy.

In the coming chapters, we'll cover:

- the financial basics so that you have a better understanding of all things money-related.
- money mindsets and how to have a great relationship with your cash from an early age.
- how to earn money in many different ways.
- how to budget, set financial goals, and balance what you *need* to spend your cash on with what you *want* to spend it on.

- the skills required to make your money grow while you sleep.
- what expenses, insurance, and taxes are, and why it's essential to budget for them.
- how to build good credit without falling into common debt traps.
- how to adapt and become agile when unexpected costs come up.
- and so much more!

But before we move on to our first chapter and the information that can improve your life, one more burning question needs to be answered. "What qualifies me to give my readers advice?"

My name is C.K., and I've had a long and successful career in psychology. I started working as a case manager for Big Brothers/Big Sisters, moved into the classroom of a residential treatment center for teens and ended up counseling older teens and young adults who were homeless. While counseling teens, I came to realize that one of the most common reasons for their anxiety is money—or, more specifically, not knowing enough about money to move confidently into independence.

While there is a time and place for talk therapy, I am a solutions-driven kind of guy. So, I began to look for ways to explain finances to teens so that the anxiety they were feeling would turn to excitement for a bright financial future. It took some time and research, but eventually, I developed a learning model that works—and works well! It's called the Financial Independence Ladder.

You see, most teens are driven by a deep desire to become independent from their parents or adult guardians. They want to know that they can move out and thrive on their own or go away to college, graduate, and live a successful life. What I discovered is that most teen finance advice focuses on the *what* and *how* of money, but what teens really want to know is the *why*.

Why do we need to budget? Why save? Why rent or own a home? Why invest? The list is practically endless, and these are the questions I will answer for you. You'll receive practical advice using the Financial Independence Ladder as a framework and understand why this information matters.

The world is different from what it was when our parents grew up, and it will be a different place for our kids when we reach that stage of our lives. Providing the *why* allows every one of us to define success for ourselves and work toward this success with renewed motivation and a burning passion for reaching our goals.

So, with introductions now done, let's get down to business and begin with your *Simplified Guide to Earning, Budgeting, Saving, Investing, and Creating a Positive Money Mindset for Lifetime Success and Financial Independence.*

CHAPTER 1

THE LANGUAGE OF MONEY
AND A POSITIVE MONEY
MINDSET

M indset... a word that is used quite frequently in the modern world but often isn't explained. Creating a positive or healthy mindset extends to all areas of our lives. But what is mindset?

Simply put, our mindset is how we think or feel about anything. As people, we have a mindset about our abilities, relationships, possible careers, money, and so much more. It can limit us or propel us to success! Mindset toward anything is formed by several factors, including our beliefs, what others have told us, our experiences, and how educated we are on something.

The key to understanding the language of money and building a positive money mindset while we're in our teens is knowledge, and this knowledge is called financial literacy.

Money Matters: Understanding the Core of Financial Literacy

Before we can discuss money mindsets and how to shift our perspectives about money, we first need to dive into the world of financial literacy. In the U.S., most young adults live from paycheck to paycheck. The latest stats show that 75% of teens aren't confident in their financial knowledge, and more than half of all American teens fail a basic financial literacy test (Rose, 2023).

These stats are scary because, as teens enter adulthood without financial literacy, they're more likely to make big mistakes with their hard-earned cash—but more on that a little later. For now, let's define financial literacy.

To be literate in anything, we must have both the knowledge and the skills required to make good, informed decisions. Financial literacy, therefore, is the knowledge and practical application of what we have learned to ensure our financial security now and in the future. In other words, we need to know what borrowing, debt, investing, saving, and so on are if we're going to be able to make the right financial decisions for ourselves and develop a good money mindset.

Outside of a secure financial future, financial literacy ensures that we are not falling into debt traps that can cost us everything we've worked for, allows us to accumulate assets, and has our money work for us (even when we are asleep).

The first significant investment we can make is in learning about money and becoming financially literate—your education and knowledge are *the* most important investments you'll ever make!

The Six Principles of Financial Literacy

Having our money work for us sounds amazing—right? Now that we know the difference in key financial literacy terms, we need to understand how to take everything we learn from this book and translate it to financial independence. This journey to becoming financially free begins with the six principles of financial literacy— earning, saving, investing, protecting, spending, and responsible borrowing.

Let's break these six principles down before we begin decoding dollars.

Earning

When we trade our skills, knowledge, or goods for money, we earn an income. There are many ways to make money, including a job, side hustle, business ownership, investments, assets, etc. How we earn an income is up to us, but we must get our income from different sources. This is called diversifying income, which is a fancy way of saying, "Gaining money from many different sources."

Saving

Money that is put away and not used is called saving. Now, we're not talking about stashing cash under our beds here (although this is still saving)! Proper saving is the art of putting a percentage of what we earn away in an account or investment that will grow our money over time.

Investing

Investments are different ways in which we can grow our money. An investment can be in certain commodities (in-demand resources), assets (like buildings), businesses, stocks (portions of a company), and so on. We'll do a deep dive into investments in a later chapter.

Protecting

We can protect our money and ourselves from financial loss by learning to budget properly, becoming financially disciplined, creating emergency savings, being adequately insured, borrowing wisely, etc. Protecting our money is essential for our financial well-being, and it provides us with a safety net in case something goes wrong.

Spending

Spending doesn't refer to wildly splashing our cash around. Instead, spending ties in with saving, investing, and protecting and ensures we spend our money wisely, don't fall into consumer traps (spending money on stuff we don't really need or want), and always have some money for ourselves—no one wants to work and have no fun!

Responsible Borrowing

Our final principle of financial literacy is responsible borrowing. We'll discuss this in more detail in a later chapter. For now, though, think of responsible borrowing as a way to purchase large-ticket items such as cars, homes, college tuition, etc. Paying these loans off on time is the best way to build a credible reputation with banks, other lenders, and credit bureaus.

Okay, so why are these principles of financial literacy important?

Once we become financially literate, we begin to understand the value of money and how it works. We can make great decisions for our financial future and begin to build whatever our definition of wealth is. We can also avoid making big financial mistakes like not managing our debt properly and reducing our financial vulnerability. All of this allows us to become financially independent and resilient so we can overcome any challenges we face, bouncing back like a financial pro.

Decoding Dollars: Making Sense of Financial Terms

Financial literacy may not seem like a big deal right now—I mean, most of us have quite a while until we retire—but becoming financially literate is a lifelong journey. To manage our money well, develop an excellent money mindset, and set ourselves up for a healthy financial future where we're financially independent, we must learn how to decode dollars now.

We need to learn about money (and all the different ways we can make and manage it) because we must first gain some smarts to develop a positive mindset about our cash or financial future. Mindset is about perception, and for us to challenge our perceptions, we need the facts, so let's start learning about some common financial terms.

Term	Explanation
Assets	An item or resource that has monetary value. Assets can be tangible (physical) or intangible (not physical).
Budget	A financial plan or roadmap for spending and saving. Sticking to a budget keeps expenses under control and increases savings.
Savings	Money that is set aside to achieve future goals or fulfill future needs.
Debt	Money that is borrowed from someone else, usually a bank. This money needs to be paid back with an extra fee called interest.
Credit	Your ability to borrow future money based on your income and how likely you are to pay money back.
Credit score	A number that is used to show how credit-worthy you are. This number is calculated on your borrowing and payment history, current debt, and other criteria.
Entrepreneur	Someone who starts, purchases, and manages a business.
Expenses	Money that must be spent on needs. Expenses can include debt owed, bills, services, gas, etc.
Income	Money that is earned by exchanging services, skills, or goods, or money received from investments and gifts.
Insurance	An agreement with a company to replace or pay you for specific lost or damaged items. Insurance can cover assets like a car, house or everyday goods like a laptop and cell phone.

Interest	The extra money that needs to be paid on a borrowed amount. Interest can also be *earned* on savings left in an account and on investments.
Investment	Money that is put into assets or organizations so that the money can grow.
Liabilities	Debt or money that needs to be paid to others.
Loan	Money that is borrowed from someone that needs to be paid back.
Compound interest	A type of interest earned or accumulated on both the capital (initial) amount and the fees or interest.
Stocks	A part share in a company that entitles the buyer to profits made by the company.
Taxes	Compulsory payments made to the government to cover services provided by the government.
Bonds	Money that is loaned to the government, an organization, or municipality that is paid back with interest.

Unraveling Misconceptions About Teen Money Skills

We now know a little more about money, which means we can begin to shift our mindset. But first, we need to discuss self-limiting beliefs. These are ideas or thoughts we hold onto that prevent us from reaching greatness.

For teens, these self-limiting beliefs come from things we've heard from adults, our experiences, a lack of knowledge, and, a lot of the time, fear. To send our limiting beliefs packing, we must first examine them and then uncover the facts.

Myth: I can't be successful because of my background.
Fact: Your background may present certain challenges but doesn't determine your ultimate success. Many successful individuals have overcome adversity and achieved their goals despite their backgrounds.

Myth: I'm bad at math, so I can't be good with money.
Fact: Math isn't everyone's strong point, but you only need basic math to learn how to budget and grow your money.

Myth: The Bank of Mom and Dad will always be open.
Fact: Your Mom and Dad will be a financial safety net for a bit longer, but not forever. Relying on the Bank of Mom and Dad can prevent you from becoming financially independent or moving into adulthood.

Myth: Credit cards permit unlimited spending without conse-quences.
Fact: Credit cards come with a limit, and you need to repay the money you've spent within a short period. Not paying your credit card payment on time and in full can ruin your financial reputation with lenders.

Myth: Credit cards and debt are bad.
Fact: Credit cards and debt are not all bad. What counts is how you handle your credit cards and debt by managing how much debt you have and how well you pay it off.

Myth: You need a lot of money to start investing.
Fact: You can start investing with very little money. There are plenty of low-cost, low-risk investment options available to new investors.

Myth: I'm young; financial blunders won't affect my future.
Fact: The financial decisions you make while you're young may not be catastrophic, but they can form bad financial habits you will battle into adulthood. Developing good financial habits should be your priority right now.

Myth: I should only save what's left at the end of the month.
Fact: You should be contributing to your savings as part of your monthly budget every month. This means your savings amount is paid at the same time as your other needs expenses.

Myth: Wealth requires a large salary.
Fact: Wealth requires financial literacy and capability. Some of the wealthiest people in the world came from very poor, underprivileged families.

Myth: More money equals more happiness.
Fact: Happiness comes from achieving your goals and living a life that aligns with your values and purpose. While having money makes achieving these goals easier, it's not the source of happiness.

Myth: Teens can't learn about finance.
Fact: You're never too young to learn about money and finances. In fact, the younger you begin, the earlier you can become financially independent.

Myth: There will be time to be financially responsible later.
Fact: There may be time later, but not learning about finances now can cost you a lot of cash earned in compound interest.

Myth: Teens are too young to earn money.
Fact: In the U.S., teens can legally work for an employer from age 14. There is no age limit on when you can start a business and earn money for yourself on other platforms.

Myth: Schools will teach everything about money.
Fact: Currently, less than 25 states offer financial literacy programs in schools. You can't rely on your school to teach you about money and finance.

Myth: Retirement is an older adult's concern.

Fact: The longer you don't think about your retirement, the less money you will have for your retirement. No one is asking you to imagine being old, but you should imagine yourself wealthy and financially free.

Shifting Perspectives: Shifting Your Views On Money

Many teens grow up thinking that money is either good or bad. The reality is that money is neither good nor bad; it's simply a tool to achieve your goals and a medium of exchange. For example, would you think of your vacuum as good or bad? Chances are you think of it as a tool to clean your room when it's dirty—right? Money can be used in whatever way you want it to be used. It's as simple as that!

So where does the saying, "Money is the root of all evil" come from then?

Well, first of all, that saying is misquoted all the time. The actual saying states, "The *love* of money is the root of all evil." What this means is that greed and, more specifically, an unhealthy relationship with money can lead people to make bad decisions about earning and spending money.

So, money can be used as a tool for both bad and good, and it begins with becoming financially responsible and building a healthy money mindset.

Negative Money Beliefs

Teenagers' negative money beliefs are limiting and can prevent them from achieving their goals in life. Most of these beliefs come from things we've heard or read. These beliefs implant themselves in our subconscious mind and end up holding us back.

Now look, it's not uncommon to think about money being evil or difficult to come by or that we're not destined to be wealthy. But, if these thoughts stop us from learning about money or drive us to spend our cash irresponsibly, then we need to do the work to overcome them. Creating and sustaining wealth will be nearly impossible if we approach money with nagging thoughts or if our behaviors are driven by fear.

We need to free our minds of these negative thoughts and beliefs so we can transform our perceptions. Then, we can begin making, saving, and investing money and prove to ourselves that we deserve to be successful in life. So, how do we begin to unravel our money mindset and change our minds about making and accumulating moolah?

1. Begin by uncovering any limiting beliefs you're holding on to. Think about what you've heard about money and whether or not you believe them to be true.
2. Ask yourself what your family and parents' attitudes are towards money. Do they budget? What kinds of conversations do they have about money? Do they even talk about money?
3. When you think about money, how do you feel? Do you feel anything at all?
4. Are you curious about money? When you are, what are your thoughts and feelings?
5. What do you think wealth or success is? Do you believe that money plays a role in wealth or success?

Now, don't worry; there are no right or wrong answers here, but chances are that if anxiety, fear, or worry arise when answering these questions, a change in money mindset is needed.

Building a Healthy, Balanced Money Mindset

We've established that most people aren't 100% balanced regarding their thoughts and beliefs about money, and that's totally okay. Money is, however, a factual thing—a tool that can be used to trade for things we need and to achieve our goals.

In order to build a healthy money mindset, we need to detach our emotions from it to create a more balanced perspective. (I mean, we don't have any strong emotions about our vacuum, do we?) Some of the emotions we can experience surrounding money include greed, fear, anxiety, excitement, joy, or even the fear of missing out (FOMO). While not all of these emotions are negative, any emotion can potentially cloud our judgment. Yes, that's right. Even positive emotions about money can cause us to make bad decisions. Imagine being so excited about buying something that we put ourselves into debt and can't afford to pay it back!

Next, we'll need to examine our money blind spots—those small details that affect our financial confidence, like a lack of financial literacy. Once we can identify our money blind spots, we can create a list of skills and education needed. When we know what we need to become successful, we can create a roadmap for ourselves.

Finally, we can begin to rewire our brains, choosing to view money with a more balanced mindset. We can learn to tell ourselves that with proper planning and action, we will have enough money to achieve our goals. We're capable and skilled enough to succeed in our money endeavors and resilient enough to overcome any challenges or mistakes.

Money Mindset Daily Practices

Money mindset exercises allow us to practice changing our thinking. How we think about money can affect everything from how we earn it to how we choose to spend and save the cash we make.

As we now know, our beliefs and ideas about money come from what we've heard and read about it, and for us to become more balanced in our perspectives, we need to rewire our thoughts. This might sound difficult, but our thoughts and behaviors are things that we've repeated or been exposed to a lot in our lives. If we expose our brains to new information and learn and repeat this info, we can lay new neural pathways in our brains, rewiring our thoughts.

Think of it this way, when we first learned to tie our shoes or brush our teeth, we really had to think about what we were doing. However, over time and with practice, these two daily behaviors have become things we do without much thought or effort.

Creating an automatically balanced money mindset can be done the same way we do all the other behaviors we do every day without much thought—practice! Here are some exercises we can do daily to ensure we become money mindset pros.

1. **Practice gratitude**: Gratitude may sound like magic guru nonsense, but neuroscience shows that it's a super powerful tool for rewiring our brains (Brown & Wong, 2017). Being grateful for the knowledge we have gained about money and the money we have earned can help create a more balanced mindset.

2. **Analyze spending**: A lot of the time, we spend money without even thinking about other things it could be used for. For example, the average American spends $2,000

every year on coffee takeout. Imagine what we could do with $2,000! Analyzing our daily spending can help us find where our negative automatic behaviors cost us valuable cash. In finding these gaps in our spending, we can begin to save and build a more balanced approach to money.

3. **Visualize financial success**: Success is different for everyone. Some want to be business owners, others want to just live comfortably, and others may want to be uber-wealthy. The one thing all successful people have in common is that they take the time to imagine (visualize their success). Spend 10 minutes daily to see what the future looks like for you.

4. **Think about mistakes**: Taking the time to think about money mistakes we may have made can help us understand why we made them and how we can do better the next time we're faced with a similar situation. Remember, mistakes aren't something to fear—they're perfect opportunities to learn!

5. **Dedicate time for financial knowledge**: Spending 10 minutes daily to increase our financial knowledge will ensure we have the information needed to make wise decisions.

Your Balanced Money Mindset

A balanced money mindset does not involve thinking there will always be money, no matter how much we spend, or worrying about not making enough money to save. Diving headfirst into committing to a new way of living is all great, but a lot of the time, we either lose motivation or make so many mistakes that we lose hope and give up. This happens for many reasons, but the top two are that we need to *unlearn* our old behaviors and try to change too many things at once. When we try to change too many things in one go, we can overwhelm our brains. The answer to changing our money mindset is to focus on one small detail at a time—beginning with reading this book.

Okay, so before we discuss these small changes, let's define a balanced money mindset.

Having a balanced money mindset means having a healthy relationship with money. It's the ability to see money as nothing more than a tool for achieving our life goals and definition of success. This means removing any emotions we have about money. We *don't* define our self-worth by how much money we have, nor allow money to control our lives.

To achieve a balanced money mindset, we must:

- understand what money is and its role in our lives.
- learn how to earn money.
- set financial goals for ourselves and take action to achieve these goals.
- be able to differentiate between wants and needs.
- learn about budgeting and practice what types of budgets work for us.
- begin saving early.
- practice financial control and manage debt.
- get involved in discussions about money and ask questions.
- continue to grow our financial literacy.

Money Mindset Exercise

Below is an exercise that can be completed before moving on to the next chapter. Don't worry, there are no right or wrong answers. It's simply an exercise to help establish where you are on your financial literacy journey so that you know what needs some extra work and what you're already acing! Take your time and really think about your answers.

1. Where are you in your financial journey?
2. When you think about your money habits and mindset, where are you on your journey to a balanced perspective?
3. What two money mindset behaviors are you great at already?
4. When it comes to your knowledge of money, where are you on your journey?
5. What two money behaviors are you great at right now?
6. What are two things you'd like to save toward in your future?
7. What is one thing you can start to do today that will help you save enough money for the two things you listed?

Money Terms Exercise

Below is a list of common money and banking terms. Try to match each of these terms with the corresponding word. Simply assign the number of the word or phrase next to the definitions provided in the table below. Don't worry if you don't get them all right—that's why you're reading this book, to learn!

Term	Number
Something that is offered by a financial institution that allows a customer to put money in and take money out.	
Money that is in an account that is kept with the intention to grow it.	
Taking money from any bank account.	
Money that is earned or added to an original amount that was deposited or borrowed.	
The plastic card that is used to access money that is in a bank account.	
When money is placed into a bank account.	
Money that is moved from one bank account to another, even if it's not yours.	

1. Compound interest.
2. Savings.
3. Bank account.
4. Transfer
5. Debt card.
6. Withdrawal.
7. Deposit.

We've begun to decode the language of money and now have a better idea of a balanced money mindset and how we can become more optimistic about our financial future. But none of these matters if we don't know how to begin earning our first buck... so let's get into it.

CHAPTER 2

EARNING EARLY:

SECURING YOUR FIRST PAYCHECK
AND GENERATING INCOME

Teenagers have many priorities: school, sports, a social life, hobbies, and deciding on what college to attend—the list is nearly endless. Money may occasionally be on some of our minds, but it's definitely on all our minds when we don't have enough.

Most teens rely on the "Bank of Mom and Dad" when they're younger. We may get an allowance, and if we need anything else, we can negotiate (or beg) for some extra cash. The undeniable truth is that money provides us with independence, and the only way we can be 100% in control of our financial future is to make our own moolah!

Outside of gaining independence, choosing to earn our own money when we're younger will help us to:

- achieve our financial goals much quicker.
- get hands-on practical money management experience when we still have the safety net of our parents.
- gain working experience and develop our skills early in our lives.

- gain a deeper understanding of the value of money and work.

A survey on what teens spend their money on showed that some save, most buy stuff they want for themselves, some donate, and others contribute financially to their homes (Statistica, 2024). Earning our own money is super important because it allows us to become financially educated much earlier in life. When we choose to spend our paychecks wisely in our teen years, we can set ourselves up for a great financial future.

Balancing School and Work

Balancing school and work can be tricky when taking on a part-time job. On the one hand, we can really come into ourselves, allowing our strengths to shine; on the other, we can battle with having enough time for the things we want to prioritize.

Like planning our financial future, we need to prepare for any upcoming earning opportunities. These plans could include talking to our parents, a counselor, or other teens who are working. Next, we need to figure out how much time we have to work and what kind of job will work best for our current schedule. Let's look at some tips for success.

1. Before applying for a job, chat with your family about your desire to work. Discuss things like how you can balance work and school, how much support they can offer, and whether they know of any jobs available.
2. Estimate the fewest number of hours you could work at first and stick to this schedule for a while. You can always add more hours once you know you can cope.
3. Learn time management to have enough time for school, work, social life, and downtime.

4. Take care of yourself by setting boundaries and sticking to a schedule. This will ensure that you get enough sleep and still have time to hang out with your friends.
5. Consider online jobs as an employment option. Working online might be easier for some teens, especially those without driver's licenses or who cannot get a ride.

Treasure Troves of Income: Diversifying Your Earning Streams

Teens will have school obligations from Monday to Friday outside of vacation times. This makes weekend and evening jobs, as well as seasonal jobs, more viable. The good news is that these types of jobs don't require much experience and offer flexible shifts so that we can still keep up with our school work while earning money.

We can earn an income in several ways, including traditional part-time jobs, online income opportunities, passive income streams, and entrepreneurship. Let's examine each of these.

Traditional Part-Time Jobs

Traditional part-time jobs involve working for someone else. Applying for traditional part-time jobs requires us to approach organizations so that we can fill certain roles within the company.

Some part-time job options include:

- bussing tables or waiting tables
- working in retail
- cashier
- summer and winter camp work (seasonal)
- grocery store clerk
- movie theater usher
- delivery driver
- barista

This list of traditional part-time jobs is nearly endless! What we need to know about this type of work is that it's often seasonal, with positions increasing during vacations and peak holiday seasons. This is also an ideal time to work as you won't necessarily need to balance work and studies. The average seasonal wage in the U.S. is just over $18 per hour, allowing us to make just over $3,000 per month during our vacay times (talent.com, 2024).

Online Employment Opportunities

Online employment can be either with a company as traditional part-time employment or as part of a side hustle business we create. How much money we can earn online largely depends on the time we put in and the type of work we do. Some more popular online options for teens include:

- tutoring
- freelancing skills like writing on certain platforms
- managing social media accounts
- digital assistant work
- online surveys

When looking for employment online, we must ensure our safety. This means not disclosing our address or other personal information and not meeting in person. In addition, many online jobs are considered "self-employed," and our taxes become our responsibility.

Passive Income Opportunities

Passive income is money earned from doing some work upfront to establish the revenue stream. Once established, money continues to be generated from little or no work. Like online opportunities, passive income streams will require us to keep track of our income for tax purposes. Some income streams we can create from passive income include:

- creating an online course
- writing e-books
- selling photos online
- advertising on a car
- sponsored posts on social media
- dividend stocks
- song lyrics
- drop shipping

Passive income takes time to build, and we may not make a lot of money for a while. Having said that, patience and persistence with passive income opportunities can lead to a lot of money made with very little work. Remember, passive income is not money for nothing. We need to invest time, effort, or money into our passive income stream for it to make any money.

Entrepreneurship for Teens

For some of us, owning a business at a young age is exciting and an ideal opportunity to earn money on our own terms. For many American teens, entrepreneurship comes more naturally, and many teens do not even realize they're business owners. An example of entrepreneurship is being a tutor! We're not employed by a company and can use our tutoring skills to earn as much money as we want (within reason). American teens often choose to start a business or side hustle based on their:

- skills.
- strengths.
- how much time they have to spare.
- how much money they want to earn.
- what their direct community needs as a service.

By assessing these five points above, we can find a business model that makes us money without worrying about the number of shifts we need. We can set our own rates, working hours, and income.

Passive Income and Entrepreneurship for Teens

Okay, so we know that a passive income is the money earned from doing some work at the beginning of a project or job and continuing to earn with little effort on the tail end (notice how I didn't say no effort)! There are several ways to generate passive income, some of which we discussed in the section above. We must understand some key points when earning passive income or starting a business.

Before we discuss these points, we need to create or purchase an asset. This asset could be our business being run solo or with employees, through compound interest earned on our savings account every month, or by making enough money from a part-time job to purchase low-risk investments.

To start a business and earn a passive income, we need to:

- identify our specific skills and interests.
- uncover our strengths and match these up with what others need—solve a problem.
- do market research and figure out how we can supply a product or service that solves the problem we've identified.
- put together a business plan similar to a resume—check out the information in the section below.
- set aside time and be prepared to put the work in to build our future assets.
- make adjustments when we see things aren't working, and stick with things that are working.
- begin to scale up and expand our business as we grow.

Getting Your Foot in the Door: Resume Building

To apply for a job or even build our own business, we must showcase our skills and unique strengths. Potential employers want to know these details so that they can assess whether we're a good match for their company. Important information, like our experience, skills and strengths, is recorded on a resume.

Before building our resume, we must gather all the information we need. A great way to do this is to have a brainstorming session where we can write down:

- a list of websites that advertise jobs for teens.
- a list of all our social media accounts—so we can clean them up and make sure any relevant accounts are job-friendly.
- a list of courses, workshops, or skills development programs we may have attended.
- any work experience we might have.
- a list of any volunteer work, clubs, or extracurricular activities.
- our strengths and skills.
- a list of certificates, achievements, or awards.
- any software or apps we can use.

Remember, software and apps include Google Suite, any Microsoft programs we may use for school assignments, social media uploading, hashtags, and Canva.

Once we have brainstormed all the above information, we can begin building our resume. The trick to a great first impression with our resume is to keep it short, concise, and punchy, highlighting our skills and strengths.

We must be sure to select the correct resume format, deciding whether chronological, functional, or a combination of both types is suitable for the jobs you will be applying for. While our resume is definitely our moment to shine, it's better to keep it free of color and easy to read. Here are some tips.

- Use a professional font that is standard—Calibri, Arial, Georgia, Times New Roman
- Try to stick to a 12-point font, which is easy to read.
- Choose 1-inch (2.5cm) margins.
- Try to condense information to one page.
- Place personal information at the top of the page, bolding important aspects like contact details. This personal info should include:

  ○ your full name.
  ○ a professional email address.
  ○ telephone number.
  ○ the suburb and city you live in.

- After your personal info, write a professional summary that includes why you're applying for a job and what your strengths are.

What to Do if You Don't Have Experience

If this is our first time applying for work, we will only have a little experience we can list. Don't worry! Employees who hire school-going teens are not looking for a long list of working experience, but they will look for other clues about who we are and how committed we will be to the job. As first-timers, we can still create a stellar resume by highlighting:

- our top three or four achievements or roles we've held.
- any informal volunteer work we've done—mowing the neighbor's lawn, tutoring cousins or friends, doing chores for relatives, babysitting siblings, etc.
- any leadership positions—student councils, sports captains, chairing dance committees, etc.
- languages we speak.
- hobbies or interests that set us apart from others.

Once we've put together our resume, we can begin looking for work. Don't worry, I'll provide tips on how to do this. One more super-critical element to our resumes that we must keep in mind: adaptability! Although sending the same resume to multiple jobs may be easier, it could be a big mistake, and here's why: Each employer will be looking for a specific set of skills from their future employees. These skills are listed in the job description and give us valuable clues on how to help our resume stand out. When applying for a job, we should adapt our resume to match these skills—but don't lie! Delete any irrelevant skills, highlight skills that fit a job description, and ensure that a *willingness to learn* is front and center when applying for jobs that require skills we don't necessarily have.

Job Applications for Teens

With our resumes now formulated and ready to go, we can begin searching for a job. Teens have it a little easier than older generations because we don't need to go through the newspaper, nor do we *have* to go door-to-door—although this can lead to successful employment. For modern teens, the internet is our first choice for online job hunting.

We can use job listing websites like Indeed, Glassdoor, Simply-Hired, or ZipRecruiter to narrow our focus, opting for jobs specifically designed for teens. Other teen-friendly websites include Snagajob, HireTeen, and NextDoor.

Aside from specialized recruiting websites, we can use social media and networking sites like LinkedIn and platforms that link local communities, such as neighborhood Facebook pages and Twitter. Recent stats show recruiters use LinkedIn, Facebook, and Twitter as their top job advertising platforms (Wonderkind, 2024).

Preparing for Interviews

An employer impressed by our resume will contact us for an interview. This is a meeting we will have with a potential employer to get to know us and discuss job responsibilities and other aspects of the job, like pay and benefits. Interviews can be held online or in person, and we must be prepared to make an excellent first impression.

Let me begin by saying it's normal to be nervous or excited when interviewing for a job, but being prepared will ensure everything goes smoothly. Remember, the person doing the interview wants to get to know you on a personal level, so be prepared, but be real. Here are some other ways to ace an interview.

- Research the company interviewing you. Consider what you'll be doing and compile a list of questions (if you have any).
- Make sure you have a list of qualifications on hand—if applicable.
- Know what you've put on your resume. You don't need to know it by heart but want to remember the important details.
- Ask someone to practice interview questions with you.
- Make a list of things you may need for your interview and bring these with you—this could include a copy of your

resume, proof of identity, or copies of certificates and qualifications.
- Dress to express your personality, but make sure to dress to impress.
- Ask if you can follow up after your interview.

Workplace Etiquette and Professionalism

It's exciting to get a call saying, "You're hired!" We're now on our way to earning our first income. At school and home, we follow certain rules and guidelines to keep us safe and help us fit in. The same applies when we join the workforce, and we must learn basic etiquette to develop our professional skills.

New rules and guidelines may sound scary, but they're not all that bad. We've already learned much about what we need for the workplace in a school or college setting. Below are some things we can consider when entering a new place of work. We don't need to memorize this list, so don't stress!

- Don't get involved in workplace gossip.
- Treat others and yourself with respect.
- Respect other's personal space.
- Be honest and develop a reputation for integrity.
- Apologize for mistakes made and own up if you make a mistake.
- Don't take credit for someone else's work.
- Be aware of noise levels and try to limit using speakerphones or playing personal music.
- Be organized and tidy in your workspace.
- Be helpful and ask when you see someone is struggling.
- Wear appropriate clothing for your job. If you need to wear a uniform, keep it neat, tidy, and clean.

- Make sure you're wearing shoes that are comfortable to walk in but clean and acceptable for a workplace—no open shoes.
- Keep jewelry to a minimum and ensure it is appropriate for the workspace.
- Try to keep your nails manicured and clean. Certain jobs require short nails, so check with your employer about the standards.
- Be on time. Every time.
- If you have a lot of tasks and duties to get through, consider creating an electronic to-do list to help you check off items.
- Have a pen and paper handy at all times—I know digital works, but you never know.
- Take breaks throughout your day so you stay energized, but make sure they are approved by your employer.
- In meetings, don't interrupt. Stay focused and ask questions in the allotted time.
- Project a positive attitude.
- Do not share too much personal info or express opinions about political or religious beliefs.
- Make sure to handle confrontation maturely—don't get into fights at work!
- Remember the names of your coworkers. No one expects you to get it right the first time, so don't worry.
- When introduced to someone new, stand up, make eye contact, and greet the other person.
- Don't use your personal phone during work time unless it's absolutely necessary and approved by your employer. Switch it to silent and leave non-urgent calls and texts for breaks or after your shift has ended.
- Don't scroll through social media during work hours.

- If you're responsible for sending work emails, address the recipient politely. Begin emails with Dear and end with Sincerely or Regards.
- Keep emails concise and to the point.
- When receiving feedback from others, be polite and manage your emotions—no one likes to hear they may have done something wrong, but feedback helps you improve.

Many of these rules and guidelines are pretty standard, but we are bound to make mistakes occasionally—it's all part of the learning process! As long as we remember to be polite, apologize for our mistakes, and choose to be honest at all times, we can overcome any mistake we may make. When in doubt, be polite, ask questions, and be willing to learn from mentors and management.

Finding Your Ideal Job Exercise

The following worksheet will help you narrow down the type of job or business you're best suited for. Simply read the question or statement in each block, answering as best you can.

Question	Response
What subject do you enjoy most in school?	
What skills are you the best at?	
What do you think sets you apart from others?	
What are your interests away from school?	
What help or volunteer work do you like best?	
If you could choose any job, what would it be?	
Have you thought about a career path? If so what is this path?	
What are some duties or chores you enjoy doing?	
What would be the best physical surrounding to work in?	
What extra training would you like to receive for your job?	
How much money would you realistically like to earn?	
How do you think a job can help you with your future career?	

Once you have answered all these questions, look for patterns or information that might connect. For example, if you're great at communicating with younger kids, education is your passion, and you like to work in a more homely environment, babysitting, kindergarten assistant, or tutoring might be for you!

CHAPTER 3

GOAL-GETTER & MONEY-MASTER:

SETTING S.M.A.R.T. GOALS AND BECOMING A BUDGETING BOSS

We all know there are teen millionaires out there, but we often wonder how this is possible. Are these teens built differently from us? Are they lucky? Did they have a hand up? I mean, many teens aren't even old enough to get a job yet! Here's the reality, though: today's teens are more highly educated than teens ever have been (barring financial literacy), and there's a *whole* lot more information at our fingertips. How we use that information is often the difference between whether or not we become financially healthy.

Targets & Treasures: Setting Your Financial Goals

Before discussing financial goals and how we can set our own, let's examine why goals are important.

Firstly, having financial goals teaches us to be organized with our time and the tasks needed to achieve what we set out to do. By creating achievable goals, we can take small steps every day. Eventually, all of these steps will lead to a successful outcome.

Secondly, regularly achieving small milestones keeps us motivated, provides us with a sense of empowerment, and shows us that we can accomplish what we set out to do. In addition, we can begin to think with a more experienced mind because we learn from small mistakes we make along the way.

Finally, it allows us to put the skills we learn into practice. The more financially literate we become, the more empowered we become to achieve whatever our definition of success is.

Okay, now that we know the tremendous benefits of setting goals, let's uncover how to set our financial goals with the specific, measurable, achievable, realistic, and time-based (SMART) method. SMART goals can be used in any area of life, but we're learning about finance now, so let's break them down.

Specific	Your financial goal needs to be specific. You must be clear about what you want to achieve. Instead of saying I want to save money, be specific and say, I *will* save (x) amount of money every month.
Measurable	Next, you'll want to make your goal measurable. This clearly defines your goal and provides a benchmark that lets you know you're progressing.
Achievable	Once you have a measure of what you want to achieve, you want to assess whether or not your goals are achievable. Setting a goal to save $3,000 this year is pointless if you only earn $1,000 a year. If your goal isn't achievable, you're setting yourself up to fail.
Realistic	Next, you'll want to assess the steps needed to achieve your goal. Are these steps realistic? If you need to work 50 hours a week to achieve your goal and go to school, your goal isn't realistic.
Time-based	Finally, break down your time frame for each of your milestones. This will give you small goals to work toward. Remember, each small goal brings you closer to your larger goal, so focus on getting the small stuff done, and the big stuff will happen naturally.

Creating SMART Financial Goals: Your Template

Now that we know what SMART financial goals are, we can set our first financial goal. Try to make this goal small so that you can practice this newly acquired skill.

Fill in the worksheet below and take action daily to achieve your goal.

Step	Answer
Specific: Is my goal clearly defined, and does it make sense?	
Measurable: How will I know I've achieved my goal or monitor my progress?	
Achievable: How am I going to break down this goal to make sure I can achieve it?	
Realistic: Can I realistically achieve my goal and what extra help do I need?	
Time-based: How long will it take me to achieve my goal and each milestone?	
SMART statement: Put all of the information above into a statement that you can refer to when achieving your goals.	

Craft Your Short-Term and Long-Term Goals

In finance and in life, we will set goals of different lengths. These are classified as short-, mid-, and long-term goals. Short-term financial goals are goals we want to accomplish within the next three months to three years. Mid-term goals are what we want to achieve in three to five years, and long-term goals are in the next ten, twenty, or even thirty years. For teens, planning for the immediate future and up to ten years is more than enough time, so don't worry—we don't have to plan for our retirement just yet!

This is not a set practice; it is simply a standard guideline that makes sense when laying out plans. Many people plan even longer milestones, spanning 10, 20, or even 50 years. Usually, a five- or ten-year plan is sufficient, and you are always free to make changes along the way.

Tips for Short-Term Goals Setting

Short-term financial goals provide a solid foundation for our mid- and long-term goals. When setting our short-term goals, we can work backward from what we want to achieve in the future or forward, breaking down each milestone. Here are some key tips for setting our short-term goals.

- Make sure that goals are SMART. This method makes it easier to keep track of progress and ensures that you can adapt and pivot if you encounter obstacles.
- Track progress regularly to adjust and learn from any mistakes you make. During your review and tracking time, remain flexible and remind yourself that small steps are progress toward the final outcome.
- Review your short-term goals every three months and break them down month by month. Remember, you're not aiming to do 100% all at once—1% every day will eventually add up to 100%.

Tips for Mid- and Long-Term Goals

Mid- and long-term goals can be scary for a couple of reasons. On the one hand, we want to remain optimistic and motivated toward what we want to achieve in the future. On the other hand, we know that things can change as we grow and our lives change. Short-term goals are easier to achieve simply because less time is involved, meaning fewer variables. A lot can change in five or ten years, which means we should set ourselves mid- and long-term goals—here's how.

- Think about where you want to be in 10 years, then work backward from your goal. If you want to own $10 million in investments, how will you achieve this in years 9, 8, 7, and so on?
- Once you have worked these goals back into annual achievements, you can begin breaking them into monthly and even weekly milestones. This will help you transform your mid- and long-term goals into short-term goals, creating small daily practices to help you gain confidence and begin making progress.

Be On Track: Staying Motivated Toward Your Goals

We've chatted a bit about staying motivated while working toward our financial goals. Motivation is a temporary emotion. That's right —it is not meant to be maintained for a long time! Instead, it provides us with enough excitement to build self-discipline. We become motivated when our brains are rewarded by positive behavior. This reward could be feeling proud about achieving a goal milestone, seeing our bank account grow as we save, or over-coming a financial obstacle or challenge.

Conversely, not achieving our milestones or seeing time tick by without much improvement in our financial affairs can break our motivation, and we can begin to feel like setting goals makes us feel rotten. We can become motivated by:

- naming your goals, making them specific, defining what success looks like for you, and ensuring you take action and avoid the temptation of spending on things you don't need or want.
- talking about your financial success and what you want to achieve. Find friends and family members who will share in your dreams, provide you with support, and be a sounding board for you to discuss obstacles and solutions.
- learning to celebrate your small wins. It doesn't matter how small your achievements are; celebrating them will ensure your brain is rewarded for your significant financial behaviors.
- choosing to set financial boundaries and discussing these with our friends and family. Let others know that you're serious about achieving your goals and ensure you are reinforcing your boundaries.

Remember that motivation is not meant to last forever. It's designed to give us enough excitement and strength to build our self-discipline skills. Goals will provide you with direction, but you will still need to learn the skills required to achieve each of the goals and milestones you set for yourself, and that is where budgeting comes in.

The Art of Budgeting: Conquer Your Finances

Before we get into the nitty-gritty of budgeting, I want to make one thing clear: budgeting is not something we should dread or fear! It's a fantastic tool that we can use to accumulate money, achieve our goals, and build wealth over time. It lets us know where we are spending our money and where we don't *need* to spend it, *allowing* us to buy the stuff we really want.

If we want to become financially independent and free, we need to learn the basics of budgeting—it's as simple as that. So, let's examine the definition of a budget: A budget is a plan we create for spending and saving money. It provides a framework for achieving our financial goals and meeting our daily and weekly goal milestones.

How to Craft Your Budget

Creating a budget is the first step to understanding where our money goes each month and progressing toward financial independence. Part of becoming financially literate is developing the ability to craft our budget and sticking to it. Here's how.

1. **Figure out your income**: Your first step is pretty straightforward—figure out how much you're earning every month. If you are paid at different times (weekly, biweekly) or per shift, it may take you a full month to calculate this amount. For self-employed teens with fluctuating incomes, it's a good idea to look at what you earned over the last three months to find an average.
2. **Calculate your expenses**: Once you know how much you earn, you can begin to look at how much you're spending. You can do this by looking at your bank statements (and credit card statements if you have one). The trick to looking at your expenses is to go back at least three months to calculate an average. Once you know what this average is, you can break down your expenses into needs (the things you have to spend money on) and wants (the things that are nice to have).
3. **Tie your budget in with your goals**: Seeing how much you spend every month and how much money is wasted can be pretty shocking, but the good thing is it lets you know how realistic your goals are. Tying your budget in with your

goals also allows you to decide how much of your wants-spending can be diverted to savings or how this money can be better used towards your goals

4. **Pick a budgeting plan**: The 50-30-20 budget is the easiest for teens to follow, but there are many different budget plans out there. I'll break each of these down for you in the section below.

5. **Implement your budget**: Once you've assessed your spending and income and have chosen a budget, there's nothing left to do but take action. This means sticking to your budgeted amounts every month and moving your savings over to your chosen compound interest accounts.

One thing we should know about budgeting is that it's not fixed. We need to be realistic as we begin to work on achieving financial independence and understand that some adjustments will need to be made. This doesn't mean choosing to blow all your savings on a new pair of kicks! Rather, it means being flexible, tracking our expenses, and planning ahead appropriately.

It's a good idea to use an app to track expenses once you have a budget in place. This way, you can see where you may be over-spending or if there's anything you're neglecting to save for—like emergency expenses. Apps like LendingTree, EveryDollar, and 1Money can provide insight into where our money is going and help us categorize our expenses. They can also help us adjust our budgets when our income increases or decreases.

Types of Budgeting Plans for Teens

As we mentioned above, the 50-30-20 plan is one of the most manageable budgets for teens to follow. However, teens can also use a couple of other budget plans to track their income and expenses easily.

- **50-30-20**: This budget allows you to spend 50% of your income on needs like rent, utilities, and debt, 30% on wants like new clothes, streaming services, and takeout, and 20% on savings and investments.
- **Envelope budget**: This method gained popularity on social media not too long ago and involves creating an envelope for every spending category and placing cash into each of these envelopes. Once the envelope is empty, you must either take money from another envelope or go without.
- **Zero-based budgeting**: A zero-based budget can be tricky, especially for teens just starting their budgeting journey. If you have self-discipline and nerves of steel, try to give this budgeting plan a go. Assign every single dollar you earn to each of your categories. If you're going to try this method out, make sure to budget for emergency savings as well as regular savings and money for investments

Deciphering Needs From Wants in Your Financial Journey

Once we've chosen our chosen budget, we need to separate our needs from our wants—this can be tough when we've convinced ourselves that we *need* that new pair of kicks. So, how do we separate what we need versus what would be nice to have?

Let's begin with the definition of both these words. A *need* is something necessary to live and function on a day-to-day basis. Needs include food, shelter, medicine, clothing, heat, water, etc. *Wants* are things that can improve our quality of life. We may *need* new clothes, but we *want* more expensive, branded clothing.

- Pro tip for separating wants from needs: Let 24 hours pass before buying something. If we feel stronger the next day about a purchase, chances are it's a need. Extending the time even further and assessing how we feel will let you really know if it's a need or a want.

Remember, every teenager's financial needs will vary based on their lifestyle, responsibilities, and personal circumstances. We must prioritize needs over wants and allocate money to savings based on what we are capable of right now, adjusting our budgets as we build more money and our lifestyles change.

Unhealthy Spending: Common Spending Mistakes You Should Avoid

As we can see from the budgeting information above, a budget still allows us to spend money on wants, so we're not depriving ourselves of what we want every month. However, we must remember that we mustn't just spend for the sake of spending, which can be tough when trying to keep up with our friends and fit in.

In addition to wanting to fit in and experiencing FOMO, we can find ourselves spending cash out of habit—this can be *super frustrating* when we're trying to change our money habits. We need to become mindful of our spending and avoid some common spending mistakes if we're going to make our budget work—here's how.

- **Excessive spending**: Large amounts of money are lost and gained one dollar at a time, and while that $2 coffee might not sound like a big deal now, it all adds up. The average American spends around $2,000 yearly on takeout coffee alone (Rosenfeld, 2021). The tips below can help us save on these small "dollar" purchases and begin accumulating wealth instead of spending it.

- **Not keeping track of our spending**: Losing track of our finances is a common mistake. It's a good idea to check bank accounts frequently to ensure we're on track with our budgeted amount and manage our money correctly.
- **Not sticking to our budget**: Creating a budget is great, but we can quickly fall into bad spending habits if we don't commit to positive financial action. Remember, every time we go off budget, we prolong our healthy financial future, so stick to it!
- **Paying minimum amounts**: For those of us with credit cards and loans, paying the minimum amount can sound appealing. Here's the thing about debt: using it responsibly can help us build a healthy financial future, but using it irresponsibly can lead us down a seriously troubled path. Paying extra on our loans shortens the repayment time and ensures we become debt-free much quicker.
- **Not saving for emergencies**: Life happens, and when an emergency hits, we must have the funds to cover it. Now, emergency savings doesn't mean just saving for the big stuff like getting sick or having accidents. We're talking fridge repairs, blown car tires, and laptops suddenly deciding to stop working. Not having emergency funds can set us back financially, sometimes taking years to recover.
- **Not controlling impulse buying**: I get it! We all go into the store and get tempted by shiny displays and new gadgets, but we need to use the 24-hour rule to cool off before we commit to a purchase. Taking a day or two to decide whether a purchase is worth it can really help put things into perspective.
- **Not being aware of emotional spending**: Emotional spending often happens when we don't have a better money mindset. Sometimes, we spend money when we are stressed or sad, other times when we are happy or "deserve a treat." Spending money to make us feel better about

ourselves can lead us into debt, so it's wise to avoid it entirely. Instead, take the time to practice self-care and uncover what is causing the need to spend.

Strategies to Overcome Unhealthy Spending

Knowing the common mistakes we make when it comes to spending is one thing. Still, we need to learn how to overcome any unhealthy spending habits we may have. Before we look at these strategies, though, we must acknowledge that overcoming anything unhealthy in our lives comes down to how we think and feel—so pay attention to the money mindset at all times!

Now, let's look at how we can gain more control over our unhealthy spending.

- Shop intentionally and make use of discounts, coupons, and specials. Always remember, if you wouldn't pay full price for an item, it's probably something you didn't need.
- Commit to cooking at home at least five days a week. The money spent on delivery fees for takeout alone can save you a lot of money every month.
- Don't quit everything all at once! Trying to give up all of your bad spending habits at once can feel overwhelming, and you could end up miserable about your newfound financial freedom. Instead, look at the "big ticket" items (the stuff costing you a lot) and decide which of those costs you'll get rid of first.
- Be mindful about what you're spending and what you're feeling when it comes to spending money. Remember that money shouldn't make you feel anything because it's just a tool to achieve your goals.

- Take a look at what triggers you to spend, especially when you're shopping online. Habits will always come with a trigger. If you uncover those triggers, half of your battle against your bad money habits will be won.
- In the beginning phases of your budgeting journey, consider drawing cash from an ATM so that you know exactly how much money you have to spend. But don't be tempted to go and withdraw more cash!
- If you're nervous about having cash, choose to move your wants spending money over to a separate debit card so that you're not accidentally dipping into your savings and needs budget.

Budgeting Worksheet

Monthly Income	Amount
After-tax salary or wages	$
Allowance	$
Side hustles	$
Any other income	$
Total Income	$
Needs (monthly)	**Amount**
Rent/mortgage	$
Homeowners' or renter's insurance	$
Auto insurance	$
Health insurance	$
Out-of-pocket medical costs	$
Electricity and natural gas bill	$
Water bill	$
Sanitation/garbage bill	$
Groceries, toiletries, and other essentials	$

Car payment	$
Parking and registration fees	$
Car maintenance and repairs	$
Gasoline	$
Public transportation	$
Phone bill	$
Internet bill	$
Student loan payments	$
Credit card payments	$
Other	$
Total Needs	**$**
Wants (monthly)	**Amount**
Clothing, jewelry, etc.	$
Eating out	$
Special meals at home	$
Movie and concert tickets	$
Gym or club memberships	$

Travel expenses (not daily travel)	$
Cable or streaming packages	$
Home decor	$
Other	$
Total Wants	**$**
Savings (monthly)	**Amount**
Emergency fund contributions	$
Savings account contributions	$
401(k) contributions	$
Individual retirement account contributions	$
Other investments	$
Other	$
Total Savings	**$**
Total Expenses (Needs+Wants+Savings)	$
Income Remaining (Total Income – Total Expenses)	$

With your goals set, a proper budget in place, and a commitment to taking action, you can begin to become a master of your finances! Like everything else in life, though, to become a master, you must first level up your skills and know the ins and outs of taxes, insurance, and bills.

CHAPTER 4

MASTERING MONEY MOVES:

THE COOL TEEN'S PLAYBOOK TO TAXES, INSURANCE, AND MONTHLY BILLS

T axes are money we pay (contribute) to the local, regional, or national government. Get used to them—Benjamin Franklin (the face of the $100 bill) once said the only two guarantees in life are death and taxes! This money is used to finance the government to pay for all the goods and services we receive. These services include public schools, police and emergency services, Medicare, building and upkeep of roads, water and sanitation services, maintenance of public spaces and national parks, social security programs, and so much more.

In the U.S., taxes are applied to our income, some of the things we buy, like fuel, and some adult items like alcohol and cigarettes. For the most part, taxes in the U.S. are applied to the money we earn from our salary or wage, capital gains, interest earned, and other incomes—let's take a look at the most common taxes.

- **Income tax**: A percentage of our earned income paid to the federal or state government.
- **Payroll tax**: A percentage held back by an employer who pays this amount to the government to fund Medicare and Social Security programs.
- **Sales tax**: The tax applied to some goods and services—differs from state to state.
- **Property tax**: A percentage applied to the value of land, including the buildings on the land.
- **Capital gains tax**: A percentage applied to the sale of an asset like a house, property, stocks, or bonds.

The Basics of Taxes for Teens

Let's answer the obvious question first—do teens need to file a tax return? Well, the answer is a bit complex. Some teens do, and some don't, but all teens over 18 who earned income need to file. As of 2023, any minor (under 19) who earns less than $13,850 does *not* have to pay taxes separately from their parents. Even then, we may still need to file our taxes based on whether or not we're dependent. If you're a dependent of your parents, they will claim you and take the deduction. So, make sure you discuss this with your folks before filing. The IRS doesn't like double dippers!

We are considered dependent minors if we are under the age of 19, if we're going to school full-time if we live with our parents for more than half the year, and if we contribute less than 50% of our earnings to our household every year. However, we must still file a tax return if our earnings exceed the threshold.

The criteria for us to be independent include:

- How much money we earn—over or under $13,850.
- How much unearned income we accumulate in a year.
- How much combined income we earn—unearned plus earned income.

I strongly encourage everyone to file their taxes, even if we don't need to, so we can better understand the process when we do have to file—here's how.

Step 1: Add Up Your Income

Add up your income to determine whether or not you need to file your tax return. If you have made more than the minimum permitted amount, you'll need to file it. (I'll break down each form for you in the section after this one.)

Step 2: Get Your Documents Together

If you're going to file a tax return, you'll need to provide some information. This includes your:

- social security number.
- W-2s from your employer.
- 1099 if you're self-employed.
- 1099 if you have made money from an investment.
- any receipt of expenses for your side hustle or business, if you have one.

Step 3: Choose Your Tax-Filing Software

Some people still prefer to fill out paper tax forms, but that takes more time. Most use one of the IRS software programs to help you file your taxes online. Some software programs charge a fee, so be sure to pick one that is right for you. The list of authorized software programs is on the IRS website.

Step 4: Complete Your Return

Once you have chosen your software, you can begin filing your tax return. Be sure you set aside some time to do this because it can take up to an hour. When you're filling in your form, you will need to:

- start with your basic info.
- choose your filing status.
- report all of your income earned.
- choose from the list of deductions available—make sure you have proof. For teens, this includes education and business items.
- select tax credits—most software programs will do this for you automatically.
- sign your return and submit it.

Once you have submitted your taxes, you will receive a notice informing you if you will receive a refund or need to pay taxes. If you're owed a refund, the quickest way to get paid is to select the direct deposit option.

After you have filed your federal tax return, you need to file your state tax return as well. Your software can transfer all your information to your state tax return forms for you.

If you owe taxes, you must pay the amount owed to the state or IRS by the deadline. Not paying taxes can cost you even more money in interest and penalties. The easiest way to pay taxes is to pay them directly through your bank account or write a check.

Tax Forms and Lingo Made Easy

Tax forms can be intimidating. All those new terms and lingo can make it feel like we're reading a completely different language—and we're expected to understand it! Let's decode these words so that you can begin to understand what you're reading and filling in.

- **W-2 Form**: This is also known as a Wage and Tax Statement. It is a document that an employer needs to send to their employees and the IRS. This form reports your annual earnings and how much tax has been withheld on them. W-2 forms are only for employees who earn money from an employer who deducts taxes and sends these taxes to the government.
- **W-4 Form**: This form is required if you work directly for an employer and tells the employer how much tax should be withheld from your paycheck. Factors like marriage, joint returns, whether you have any dependents, and how many jobs you work will all affect your tax contributions.
- **1099 Miscellaneous Income**: A 1099 form reports income not directly earned through an employer. Because there are many different ways to make money outside of a traditional job, there are several types of 1099 forms.
- **1098 Student Loan Interest**: This form reports how much interest you paid on student loans in the last year. Your loan service provider will send you this form if you paid over $600.
- **Deductions**: A tax deduction reduces your taxable income. Standardized deductions are set at a fixed amount, and itemized deductions are usually reserved for higher-income earners with many expenses to deduct.

- **Credits**: Money you can subtract from the taxes you owe is called a credit. These credits will differ from person to person but are used to lower your taxable income.

With tax terminology now mastered, we need to demystify your paycheck and pay stub so that you can stay ahead of your taxes and know exactly how much to budget.

Understanding Your Paycheck and Pay Stub

The words paycheck and pay stub are often used interchangeably, but there are some key differences in their definitions and uses. Let's start with your paycheck. This is a physical paper check made out to you for the work you have done. In the U.S., only about 4% of workers still get a paper paycheck (Leonard, 2020). Most employees will receive their wages or salary through an automated payroll platform directly to their bank account.

On the other hand, your pay stub provides you with a summary of all the amounts that make up your wages. Your pay stub will include:

- Your employer and your addresses.
- Your pay date.
- The dates you worked.
- Your pay rate per hour or year.
- Your total pay (gross) and your pay after deductions (net).

Suppose you're one of the 4% of Americans who still receives a paycheck. In that case, you'll need to check that the information on the check is valid, keep the paper check safe until you can deposit it at the bank, wait until the check clears (about two days), and then use your money according to your budget.

For those of us who receive our pay directly to a bank account, you need to make sure your banking information is correct and valid, wait for the clearance period (should be automatically available), and use your money according to your budget.

Reading Your Pay Stub

Your pay stub will show not only what you have earned but also your deductions. Knowing how to read your pay stub will help you understand how much you can expect to receive in your bank account and how much tax you pay. The deductions on your pay stub will include:

- Any unpaid leave you might have taken.
- Your income tax percentage based on how much you earned.
- Social Security and Medicare deductions—if you qualify.
- Any other deductions, such as state and local income tax, unemployment insurance, health insurance, 401K, etc.

Your employer is responsible for reporting deductions on your pay stub and collecting and forwarding the amounts you have taken to the IRS and state and local tax agencies. If you feel something is wrong with your pay stub, immediately speak with a payroll representative or a your supervisor to guide you.

When creating your budget, it's important that you're working with your take-home (*net pay*) after deductions so that you can assign your money to the income category properly.

Common Tax Mistakes to Avoid

Taxes might seem like a total snooze fest, but they're essential for the country and your financial future. The software can help with the math when it comes to filing your taxes, but it's still up to you to avoid these common mistakes while filing:

- **Filing too late or too early**: You can't file your taxes late because that will cost you penalties, and filing too early can lead to processing delays. Be sure you file in the prescribed timeframe (mid-March to Mid-April) so you have all of your paperwork.
- **Missing or inaccurate Social Security numbers (SSN)**: Your SSN is essential for your tax return because it lets the government know who is filing. Be sure you type your number exactly as printed on your Social Security card. The same goes for your name—it must match your name precisely on your SSN card.
- **Entering information incorrectly**: Everything you report on your form regarding your earned income needs to be as accurate as possible. Tax software helps with this, but be careful.
- **Selecting the wrong filing status**: Don't guess when it comes to your tax status! If you're unsure, use the interactive tax assistant on the IRS website to help you choose the correct status.
- **Math mistakes**: Number mistakes happen, so make sure you double-check your math!
- **Figuring out credits or deductions**: Even the most seasoned tax filers get confused when it comes to credits and deductions. Make sure you use proper software to help calculate these credits and deductions.
- **Incorrect bank account numbers**: Oops! This is a big mistake—one you want to avoid. Be sure you're using the correct routing and account numbers on your tax return.
- **Unsigned forms**: One of the most common mistakes people make is not signing their tax forms. An unsigned tax return isn't valid, so make sure you're signing on the dotted line.

Insurance Basics for Teens

Most teens are unaware of what insurance is until they buy their first car and need to sign a document that says they need to pay for auto insurance to cover in case of an accident or loss. Now, I know, getting insurance and having to pay over some of your hard-earned money for something that hasn't happened or might never happen doesn't sound like a lot of fun. Still, insurance is a big deal—and I'll tell you why in a little while.

For now, I'd like you to think of insurance as a safety net that protects you financially when things go wrong. It's a superhero in your corner, ready to swoop in and save the day—or at least your wallet—when you're least expecting it. In the U.S., there are several different types of insurance, some of which will apply to you now and some later in life.

- **Auto insurance**: If you're driving, auto insurance is a mandatory. It covers you if you get into an accident, causing damage to your car or someone else's, or if you injure someone. Without insurance, you could be left paying a massive bill out of pocket—yikes!
- **Health insurance**: Health insurance helps cover the costs of medical care, like doctor visits, medications, and hospital stays. Healthcare in the U.S. can be really expensive, especially if you have to pay for it without insurance.
- **Renter's insurance**: This one might not apply to you just yet, but if you're planning to move out and rent a place, renters insurance protects your belongings in case of theft, fire, or other covered events. It's pretty affordable and can save you a lot of money if something happens to your stuff.

- **Life insurance**: I know thinking about life insurance might seem a bit heavy, but it's important to consider, especially as you get older. Life insurance protects your loved ones financially if something happens to you.
- **Travel insurance**: If you're planning a big trip, travel insurance is a smart move. It covers trip cancellations, lost luggage, medical emergencies, and emergency evacuations. Travel insurance is especially important if you're going overseas, where your regular health insurance might not cover you.

Okay, so how does insurance work? You pay a set amount of money, called a premium, to a registered, authorized insurance company. This premium can be paid monthly or yearly. In return for your premium, you are covered for the costs of certain events outlined in a contract you receive called a policy.

When getting insurance, it's important to shop around, not just for the best price but also for the best coverage for your needs and budget. Make sure you are asking tons of questions when shopping around so that you know exactly what you're signing up for.

Auto Insurance Essentials

Auto insurance is crucial for anyone who gets behind the wheel of a car. First things first, car insurance is often mandatory in the U.S., and driving anywhere without it could land you in trouble with the law. Not having auto insurance can result in fines, license suspension, registration suspension, and even jail time, so it's in your best interest to make sure you're adequately insured.

Aside from protecting yourself from getting in trouble with the law, having auto insurance helps protect you financially by covering the costs of any loss or damage to your car or someone else's property. If you're leasing a car or paying off a car loan, your lender or leasing agent will require you to have auto insurance. They want to ensure their investment is protected in case of an accident.

But auto insurance doesn't just protect your car. It also protects the people inside it. If you have passengers in your vehicle and get into an accident, auto insurance can help cover their medical expenses. Additionally, suppose you're in an accident, and it's your fault. In that case, auto insurance helps cover your legal fees and any settlements or judgments against you.

Auto insurance policies offer several options, and you must understand each to know precisely what your coverage is. Coverages include:

- **Liability coverage**: Covers damages you cause to others in an accident and includes bodily injury liability, injuries to others and property damage liability, damage to other people's property. Liability coverage is required by law in most states.
- **Uninsured/underinsured motorist (UM) coverage**: Protects you if you're in an accident caused by a driver who doesn't have insurance or doesn't have enough insurance to cover the damages.
- **Personal injury protection (PIP)**: Covers medical expenses and lost wages for you and your passengers after an accident, regardless of who's at fault. You'll need to find out if PIP is required in your state.
- **Medical payment coverage**: This optional coverage covers medical expenses for you and your passengers after an accident, regardless of who's at fault. It's similar to PIP but with more limited coverage.
- **Comprehensive and collision coverage**: Comprehensive coverage protects your car from non-accident damages, like theft, vandalism, or natural disasters. It will pay for

damages to your vehicle after an accident. It is required if you bought your car with a loan or if you are leasing.

The cost of auto insurance depends on a couple of factors, such as:

1. Your age and driving experience.
2. The type of car you are driving.
3. Where you live.
4. Your credit score—don't worry, I'll explain this to you in a later chapter.
5. The type of coverage you have selected.
6. Your deductible amount—how much your portion of a claim is.
7. Other non-driving factors like your gender or any medical conditions you might have.

Remember, insurance policies can be customized to fit your specific needs and budget. Work with your insurance agent to find the right balance of coverage and cost for you.

Homeowner's and Renter's Insurance

Younger teens probably don't think about homeowner's and renter's insurance, but if you're considering moving out on your own, you'll need to know about these two types of insurance.

Let's begin with who needs these types of insurance: If you own a home or a condo, then you will need homeowner's insurance, and if you're renting a space from someone else, you'll need renter's insurance.

Homeowner's insurance covers damage to a property you own, including the land and structure, as well as the personal property and liability for injuries or damages that occur on your property.

Renter's insurance will cover your personal property and liability for injuries or damages that occur on your rented property. Your landlord will be responsible for the building itself by paying home-owner's insurance.

The cost of these two insurances vary, but homeowner's insurance is usually more expensive than renter's insurance. This is because your homeowner's insurance covers many more things than renter's insurance. For renters, the insurance cost is quite affordable and can be as little as $20 per month. Discounts for security systems and other extra layers of protection apply to both homeowner's and renters' insurance, so make sure you're letting your insurance agent know about any added security you have. When choosing a policy, don't just go with the cheapest option. Make sure you have enough coverage to fully protect yourself, and read the fine print to know what isn't covered. For example, some states have separate policies for earthquakes, hurricanes, or riots.

Health Insurance Ins and Outs

Health insurance covers some or all of your medical expenses when you get sick or injured. Instead of paying all your medical bills out of pocket, you pay a monthly premium to an insurance company, and they help cover the costs. Some employers will offer some type of insurance to its full-time employees, be sure to ask if one is avail-able. There are several different types of health insurance plans out there, and we will discuss the main ones so that you know your options.

Exclusive Provider Organization (EPO): With an EPO, you can only use doctors and hospitals within the plan's network. However, you don't need a referral to see a specialist.

Health Maintenance Organization (HMO): HMOs also have a network of providers. However, you'll need to choose a primary care physician to coordinate your care and refer you to specialists when needed.

Point of Service (POS): POS plans are a mix of HMO and PPO plans. You'll have a primary care physician but can see out-of-network providers for a higher cost.

Preferred Provider Organization (PPO): PPO gives you more flexibility. You can see any doctor you want, but you'll pay less if you choose providers within the plan's network.

The most important thing is to make sure you have some form of health insurance coverage. Medical bills can add up fast; one accident or illness could put you in a financial hole if you're uninsured.

Alright, let's break down the main components of health insurance plans. Understanding these terms will help you compare plans and choose the one that's right for you.

Premiums

Premiums are the amount you pay each month to have health insurance coverage. Think of premiums as a membership fee—you pay it even if you don't use any medical services that month. Generally, plans with lower premiums have higher out-of-pocket costs when you need care, while plans with higher premiums have lower out-of-pocket costs.

Deductibles

A deductible is the amount you have to pay for covered medical services before your insurance starts to pay. For example, suppose your deductible is $1,000, and you have a $1,500 medical bill. In that case, you'll pay the first $1,000, and your insurance will cover the remaining $500. Plans with lower premiums usually have higher deductibles, while plans with higher premiums often have lower deductibles.

Out-of-Pocket Maximum

This is the most you'll have to pay for covered medical services in a year, including your deductible, copays, and coinsurance. Once you reach your out-of-pocket maximum, your insurance will cover 100% of the cost of covered services for the rest of the year. This protects you from massive medical bills if you have a severe illness or injury.

Copay

A copay is a fixed amount you pay for a specific medical service, like a doctor visit or prescription drug. For example, you might have a $20 copay for a primary care visit and a $50 copay for a specialist visit. Copays don't count towards your deductible, but they do count towards your out-of-pocket maximum.

When comparing health insurance plans, consider all of these aspects. A plan with a low premium might look appealing, but if it has a high deductible and out-of-pocket maximum, you could end up paying more in the long run if you need a lot of medical care. On the other hand, a plan with a high premium and low deductible might be a good choice if you have ongoing health issues and know you'll be using your insurance frequently.

Remember, everyone's needs are different. Take the time to understand your options and choose a plan that fits your budget and health needs. And don't hesitate to ask for help if you're feeling overwhelmed—that's what parents, teachers, and insurance advisors are for!

Reading a Pay Stub Exercise

For this exercise, you'll need to ask an adult if they have a spare pay stub available. Or, if you already have a job and receive a pay stub, you can use your own.

Grab a pen and paper and see if you can identify the following aspects of your pay stub.

1. Find your pay period.
2. Find your pay date.
3. Find your pay rate.
4. Find the number of hours you worked.
5. Find your gross pay.
6. Find your taxes or tax contributions.
7. Find other deductions made.
8. Find your net pay.
9. Find your year-to-date (YTD) earnings.

Once you have found all of these elements, answer the questions below.

1. What time frame does this paycheck cover?
2. How much do you get paid for each hour of work?
3. How many hours have you worked?
4. What was your gross pay?
5. What benefits did you receive?
6. How much money was deducted for insurance, if any?
7. What was your tax deduction?
8. What was your net pay?

Emergency Funds and Savings

While insurance is a very handy safety net, it doesn't cover every-thing. It's vital for your financial health that you have extra backup. This backup is called an emergency fund and can be a total life-saver when unexpected expenses pop up.

An emergency fund is a stash of money you set aside specifically for unexpected costs or financial emergencies. Having an emergency fund is crucial because we don't have to pay for unforeseen expenses out of pocket or from our needs and wants expenses. That's right, instead of scrambling to come up with the cash or (even worse) going into debt, you can dip into your emergency fund to cover those unexpected costs.

Now, I know what you might be thinking—saving up an emergency fund sounds hard, especially when you're already on a tight budget. But here's the thing: even small contributions can add up over time. Start by setting aside whatever you can, even a few bucks a week. As you get into the habit of saving, you can gradually increase the amount you put away.

Aim to build up an emergency fund that can cover at least three to six months' worth of your living expenses. That might seem like a lot, but having that cushion can give you some serious peace of mind. And if you ever need to tap into it, you'll be so glad you took the time to save up. In a later chapter, you'll gain some more information and insight into emergency funds. For now, try to add this to your budget; remember, every dollar counts.

Okay, you've held on through all the payments you need to make and how to budget effectively. You now know why having a safety net regarding insurance is crucial and how to create an emergency fund for yourself so you don't have to worry about financial setbacks. Now, the fun begins—formulating winning strategies so that you can start building financial security!

CHAPTER 5

SAVING GAME:

WINNING STRATEGIES FOR FINANCIAL SECURITY AND SAVING FOR BIG PURCHASES

A quick recap from Chapter 1: Your mindset is your beliefs and attitudes that shape the way you see the world and yourself. How you think is often called your perspective, and this is a pretty big deal because how you perceive things affects how you react to challenges, opportunities, mistakes, and setbacks.

There are many different types of mindsets, but the two main ones are fixed and growth. With a fixed mindset, you believe that your abilities are set in stone—if you're born smart, you'll stay smart, and if you're not, then you're not. When you have a fixed mindset, you avoid challenges or anything outside your comfort zone. With a growth mindset, you believe your abilities can be developed, and your weaknesses can be turned into strengths. You view mistakes and setbacks as temporary states that allow you to learn and grow from what has happened.

Mindset matters because it massively influences one's ability to be successful and happy in life. If you have a growth mindset, you're more likely to face new challenges head-on, persist in the face of mistakes, and achieve whatever goals you set for yourself.

The good news is that mindsets are not permanent. They can change with a little bit of practice. Regarding savings, most teens have the fixed mindset that they're not good at saving. This simply isn't true—you just haven't had enough practice yet! So, let's look at how you can gain this practice and save for your next big purchase.

A savings mindset is a way of thinking that prioritizes saving money over spending it. With a savings mindset, you always look for ways to stash your income and make it grow. A mindset geared toward saving is empowering. It allows you to set yourself up for a secure financial future when you can buy the things you need and want without sacrificing something else.

Building a savings mindset involves a variety of strategies.

1. The first step is to understand your income and what you're spending money on. Take the time to calculate how much money you actually earn and where you could cut back on spending. This will let you know how much you could be stashing away for savings.
2. The next step is setting specific financial goals—which is exactly what you did in Chapter 1. Make sure you stick to the SMART format for your goals so that you can save little bits at a time.
3. Next, you'll need to decide what percentage of your income you want to save. Remember we chatted about the 50-30-20 method of budgeting? Well, this is the percentage of savings you should aim for (20%). Having said that, if you're new to saving or working on your mindset, you may want to start smaller with 5 or 10% so that you can begin building your savings muscle.
4. Money management apps like Mint, You Need a Budget (YNAB), and Acorns can help you stay ahead of savings and stay on track with your budgets. Make sure you're

using a reliable, recommended app, and stay away from scams.

5. You may also want to boost your income by looking for ways to earn extra money. This could involve taking on a side hustle, selling stuff you don't need anymore, or getting an odd job around your neighborhood.

6. Now comes the tough one; looking for ways to cut your expenses. You shouldn't be sacrificing your quality of life, but even cutting down on takeout can save some money. You might also want to look at thrifting, taking public transport, or shopping for discounts.

7. If you plan on going to college, you can start contributing to a college savings plan now. Options like 529 plans can save you a lot of money for your future self when you need to start paying for tuition and other college expenses.

8. You could use technology to automate your savings by setting up an automatic transfer to a savings account every month. By automatically transferring to your savings, you can avoid making mistakes or accidentally dipping into your savings percentage.

9. Another great way to flex your savings muscle is to take on savings challenges. There are some challenges, like the 52-week Challenge where you save $1 in week one, $2 in week two, $3 in week three, and so on).

10. Finally, learn about investing to make your savings grow faster. Don't worry; we'll get into investing a little bit later.

Planning Your Next Big Purchase

Everyone has something big they want to buy. It could be your first car, a major investment like buying a house or condo, saving for college, or something simpler like upgrading your laptop. As a teen, we save for three common big purchases: a car, college, and our own digs (apartment or house). These three items generally cost a lot of money. While financing in the form of a loan is available, you will need to save up for deposits or down payments and have practiced money discipline to pay back your loan amounts responsibly.

- **Start early**: The earlier you start saving, the more time you'll have to reach your goal. Even if you can only put away a small amount each month, it will add up over time.
- **Set a savings goal**: Having a specific savings goal in mind will help you stay focused and motivated. Do some research to determine how much you'll need to save for your big purchase, and then break that goal into smaller, more manageable milestones.
- **Open and use a savings account**: Keeping your savings separate from your checking account can help you avoid the temptation to spend your money on other things. Look for a savings account with compound interest to maximize your savings growth.
- **Account for your other expenses**: Saving for a big purchase is exciting, but you must pay attention to your other payments. Be sure you're still sticking to your budget and meeting your regular expenses.
- **Find other income sources**: If you have trouble finding wiggle room in your budget for savings, consider temporarily increasing your earnings with a side hustle or picking up some extra shifts at work.
- **Understand the cost of your purchase**: Before you start saving, you must know exactly how much your purchase will cost. This means examining other costs involved, such as taxes, banking fees, service fees, insurance, commissions, etc.

- **Break down the costs**: To understand the cost of your purchase, you'll need to break down each of these costs. For example, if you're buying a car, you'll need to factor in insurance, maintenance, fuel, and so on.
- **Account for inflation**: Inflation is the increase in money and prices over a period of time. It fluctuates as economies go through different times, but you can work on averages. For big purchases like a house or college that may take a couple of years to save for, make sure you're adding about 2% to the current cost.
- **Do your research**: Many people get so stuck on specific options that they forget about other choices available. Make sure you're considering all your options, shop around for discounts and special offers, and consider many different financing options.
- **Create a future budget**: If you're going to get financing for these purchases, you must start working on that budget now. For example, if a car is going to cost you $200 per month, deduct this amount from your budget now and put it toward your savings.
- **Create a schedule**: Once you have a savings goal in mind, you will need to schedule your savings deductions. Popular choices for teens include weekly, bi-weekly, and monthly automatic transfers—depending on your payment schedule.
- **Remember to celebrate**: Saving for a big purchase takes time and patience. Remember to celebrate your small wins, keep your eye on the prize, and remain disciplined with your savings.

Challenges to Boost Your Savings

Savings challenges are fun ways to motivate yourself when saving for any purchase. Look at the challenges below, pick one, and stick to it to see how much money you save in a month or even a year.

1. **52-week saving challenge**: Save a little more each week for a year. Start with $1 in week one, $2 in week two, and so on. By the end of the year, you'll have saved $1,378!
2. **Track your spending challenge**: Keep a detailed record of your spending for a month. Categorize your expenses and identify areas where you can cut back and save.
3. **No-spend challenge**: Avoid non-essential spending for a set period, like a week or a month. Get creative with free activities and use up what you already have.
4. **$20 savings challenge**: Every time you receive a $20 bill, put it aside in a savings jar or envelope. Watch your savings grow with each $20 you collect!
5. **26-week challenge**: Similar to the 52-week Challenge, but condensed into six months. Double your weekly savings, starting with $1 in week one and ending with $26 in week 26, for a total of $702 saved.
6. **Coin-saving challenge**: Collect all your spare change for a set period, like a month or a year. Cash it in at the end and see how much you've saved!
7. **$5 savings challenge**: Every time you receive a $5 bill, set it aside for savings. This Challenge is more manageable for those on a tight budget.
8. **Grocery shopping challenge**: See how much you can reduce your weekly grocery bill by planning meals, using coupons, and buying generic brands. Put the difference into your savings.
9. **Investing challenge**: Learn about investing by setting aside a small monthly amount to invest in stocks, bonds, or

mutual funds. Track your progress and see how your money grows over time.

10. **Entrepreneurial challenge**: Challenge yourself to start a small business or side hustle and save all the profits. This could be anything from selling handmade crafts to offering freelance services.

11. **Debt-free challenge**: Make a plan to pay off your debt as quickly as possible. Celebrate each milestone along the way and redirect your payments into savings once you're debt-free.

12. **Long-term savings challenge**: Set a big, long-term savings goal, such as a down payment on a house or a dream vacation. Break it down into smaller monthly or yearly targets, and track your progress.

13. **Investment simulation**: Before committing to an investment, play around on a stock market simulation game to learn about investing without risking real money. Many online platforms offer free investment simulations for beginners.

Banking 101: Understanding the Essentials of Checking and Savings Accounts

Now that you know more about saving, the mindset needed to become a great saver, and how to save toward your big purchases, let's look at where your savings (and other earned income) can be stored.

We'll begin with a checking account, a type of bank account that allows you to access the money you deposit for everyday expenses. Checking accounts work by depositing cash and paychecks into your account. You can access this money by using paper checks, debit cards, or online banking facilities.

In the U.S., you must be over 13 to qualify for a teen checking account and will need an adult co-signer. These accounts usually have special features like lower fees and no minimum balance requirements. Once you are 18, you can open a checking account without an adult co-signer.

Savings accounts are also a type of bank account, but they are specifically designed to help you save money. You can open a savings account for a minor at any age, but it will still require a co-signer until you're 18. There are different types of savings accounts, including basic savings accounts, high-yield savings accounts and money-market accounts

A savings account works to grow your money because interest is applied to your deposited amount. Basic savings accounts will earn a small amount of interest, while high-yield and money market accounts typically earn higher interest. Most savings accounts have minimum balance requirements and prevent you from with-drawing over certain amounts without prior notice.

This is because savings accounts are not meant for everyday spending and transactions but to help you grow your money. Again, the type of savings account you have will depend on your specific goals, like how much you want your money to grow and how long you want to save. Most people will have both a checking and savings account to properly separate their money.

How to Choose the Right Bank Account for You

Choosing the right bank account is a big decision, but it doesn't need to be stressful. The information below can help you decide which account is best for you.

1. Look for accounts with no or low monthly maintenance, no ATM fees, or other charges. Some banks will charge no fees for students and kids, but you will need to have a minimum balance.
2. If you're under 18, you'll need to look at co-signing controls. These are the actions that co-signers are allowed to take on your account, including spending and other limits.
3. Some banks will have apps and built-in budgeting tools that help you track your spending goals and manage your money better. This feature is a big plus, especially when you're new to budgeting and saving money.
4. For a savings account, look at how much interest the bank offers on money. Choose higher-yield savings accounts that will earn you more money.
5. Branch locations and access to ATMs and online and mobile banking options are also important. Drawing cash from ATMs outside of your banking institution can be very costly, so make sure you choose a bank with easy access.

Once you have chosen your bank account, you'll need to double-check the information you have been provided. This includes:

- Understanding your responsibilities, including how much money you need to open the account, minimum balances, fees, etc.
- Asking questions about features, requirements, and fees.
- Weighing up the pros and cons for each account you are considering.
- Reviewing any other fees you might be charged, like maintenance and ATM fees.
- Asking about perks and other sign-up bonuses or rewards programs a bank has for students.
- Checking out online banking facilities and how secure and easy to use these features are.

- Staying up-to-date with features and tools a bank has to offer.

Always keep in mind that your bank account is a personal decision. While asking for advice is great, the type of account you choose is up to you and will have to fit with your financial goals.

Tips to Keep in Mind When Banking Offline and Online

Online Banking Tips

Digital and online banking is more than something cool; it's an essential part of managing your money. With online banking, you can check your balance, deposit checks, transfer funds, pay bills, manage your budget, and more. With this convenience comes a new set of risks and responsibilities, especially when it comes to keeping your personal and financial information safe from cyber-criminals and hackers. You need to keep yourself safe when banking online—here's how.

- **Use strong, unique passwords**: When creating passwords for your online banking accounts, be sure to use a mix of uppercase and lowercase letters, numbers, and special characters. Avoid using easily guessable information like birthdates or phone numbers, and never use the same password for multiple accounts.
- **Enable multi-factor authentication**: Most banks now offer multi-factor authentication. This security tool provides you with an additional form of identification, like a fingerprint or a code sent to your phone, before accessing your account. This extra layer of security can help prevent unauthorized access to your account, even if someone gets hold of your password.

- **Avoid public** Wi-Fi: I know it's super convenient to just hop online, but it's important to avoid using your online banking when linked to public wi-fi networks. These networks are often unsecured and can be easily hacked, putting your personal and financial information at risk.

- **Monitor your account regularly**: One of the best ways to catch suspicious activity early is to monitor your bank account regularly. Check your balance and transaction history often, and immediately report any unauthorized charges or transfers to your bank. Many banks also offer alerts that can notify you of certain types of activity on your account, like large withdrawals or purchases made in foreign countries.

- **Download apps from reputable sources**: If you use mobile banking apps, download them from reputable sources like the Apple App Store or Google Play Store. Avoid downloading apps from third-party websites or links sent via email or text, as these may be fake apps designed to steal your login credentials or other sensitive information.

- **Don't share your personal information**: Your bank will never ask you to provide sensitive information like your account number, Social Security number, or PIN via email, text message, or unsecured website. If you receive a message asking for this information, it's most likely a phishing scam designed to steal your identity or money.

Offline Banking Tips

Online banking is incredibly important, but sometimes, you need to visit your bank in person or use an ATM to draw cash. Just like with online banking, there are important steps you can take to make sure you're safe when banking offline.

- **Plan your bank visits**: Before you visit your bank branch, take a moment to plan your trip. Make a list of the tasks you want to do while you're there, and make sure you have all of your documents and identification ready. Avoid carrying large amounts of cash, and only visit the bank during regular working hours.

- **Review your statements**: Even if you prefer to bank offline, it's still important to review your account statements regularly. Take a few minutes each month to review your statement and check for any unauthorized transactions or errors. If you notice anything suspicious, report it to your bank immediately.

- **Protect your PIN**: When using your debit card at an ATM or in-store, always hide the keypad with your hand when entering your PIN. Avoid writing your PIN down or sharing it with anyone. If you think someone has seen your PIN, contact your bank immediately to request a new one.

- **Stay active**: If you have an account that you don't use very often, like a savings account or an old checking account, make sure to keep it active by making transactions occasionally. Inactive accounts might accumulate fees or even be closed by your bank.

- **Use your bank's ATM**: Try to use ATMs owned and operated by your bank. These machines are more likely to be well-maintained and secure, and you can avoid fees for using out-of-network ATMs. If you have to use an unfamiliar ATM, check for signs of tampering, like a loose card reader or hidden cameras.

Remember, banking in both its forms needs to be done safely to protect your money and personal information. Stay vigilant and follow the tips above to help keep yourself safe. For extra protection, chat with your bank about insurance for unauthorized access to your account.

Storing My Savings Worksheet

There are many different options available to you when it comes to saving and growing your money. The worksheet below will help you choose which of these options is best for you by weighing the pros, cons, and personal choices. Each of these options will be discussed in greater detail in later chapters, but for now, a short description has been added for you. With each option presented, you'll need to reflect on the benefits and risks, write down questions you have about an option, decide if you will place money into this option and explain your reasons.

Option	Questions	Yes or No	Reason for Choice
Certificate of Deposit (CD): A savings option from a bank or credit union. CDs have a fixed maturity date and interest rate.			
Checking account: A type of bank account where you can make deposits, pay bills, and make withdrawals.			
Health savings account: A type of account that lets you save money for medical expenses.			
Money market: An account that is federally insured. It offers a higher interest rate than traditional savings accounts.			
Savings account: An account that allows you to deposit money and offers you a set interest rate.			
U.S. savings bonds: A type of account that is issued by the U.S. government and pays a set amount of interest.			
Compound interest savings account: A savings account that provides higher interest but has lower withdrawal and minimum balance limits.			

You now have all the information you need to begin saving toward your next big purchase. You know what kinds of bank accounts are available to you and how you can keep your money safe when transacting on your account. You have many savings challenges available to you, and you have been introduced to some ways you can save to help build your savings over time.

Once you know where to stash your cash, how to have built-in security nets like insurance and emergency savings, and how to earn money, you can begin leveling up your financial knowledge and start building great credit while avoiding debt traps.

Are you enjoying what you are learning so far? Please remember to leave a review at the end of the book—for now though, let's move on to debt and credit.

SHARE YOUR INSIGHTS, SHAPE LIVES AND EMPOWER OTHERS THROUGH KNOWLEDGE

Ever thought about the ripple effect of your actions? It's profound. You see, every little bit of kindness you put out there comes back to you, often multiplied. That's the beauty of generosity.

Now, let me ask you something:

Would you lend a hand to someone you've never met, knowing you might never receive recognition for it?

Imagine this someone. They're a bit like you. Eager to get started, hungry for knowledge, yet uncertain where to find it.

Our goal is simple: to make The Ultimate Money Skills Handbook for Teens accessible to all. That's the driving force behind everything I do. But here's the catch: I can't do it alone. I need your help to reach... well, everyone.

So, here's the pitch. We all know people judge a book by its cover (and its reviews). So, on behalf of a faceless teen seeking guidance:

Could you please spare a moment to leave a review for this book?

Your gift costs nothing but a minute of your time, yet it could change the trajectory of another teen's life forever. Your review might just:

- Help a budding teen entrepreneur kick-start their venture.
- Enable a young mind to grasp the intricacies of finance.
- Provide a roadmap for someone striving for financial independence.
- Spark a journey of wealth growth and security.

To experience that warm fuzzy feeling of making a real difference, it's as simple as this: leave a review.

Just scan the QR code below to share your thoughts:

If the idea of lending a hand to an unknown teen resonates with you, then you're my kind of person. Consider yourself part of our compassionate community.

I'm even more thrilled to guide you towards a lifetime of success than you can imagine. Brace yourself for the insightful strategies and empowering lessons that lie ahead in this book.

Thank you sincerely for your contribution! Now, let's dive back into the wealth of knowledge waiting for you.

Your mentor and supporter,

C.K. Roy

PS - Did you know? Sharing something valuable with another person enhances your own value to them. If you believe this book can benefit another teen, pay it forward and pass it along to them.

CHAPTER 6

CREDIT AND DEBT:

YOUR GUIDE TO BUILDING GOOD CREDIT AND AVOIDING BAD DEBT

Credit and debt can significantly impact your financial future, but these two concepts can be confusing. You're told you need to have *good* credit, but credit cards are *bad*! Or, using credit responsibly can set you up for success, while taking on too much debt or mismanaging your credit can lead to some serious financial headaches—it's a lot to try and understand. Let's break it down so that all of this is easier to grasp before you learn *how* and *why* you should build credit and manage debt.

Good credit is the equivalent of a financial thumbs-up from lenders and creditors. Good credit means you have a history of borrowing money and paying it back on time. This borrowed money could be a credit card, a student loan, a car loan, your cell plan, or even paying your utilities on time. When you pay on time, lenders see you as a responsible and trustworthy borrower, opening up a world of financial opportunities.

Having good credit becomes your VIP all-access pass to:

- **Lower interest rates**: When you have good credit, lenders are more likely to offer you lower interest rates on loans and credit cards, saving you thousands of dollars over time.
- **Easier approval for loans and credit**: With good credit, you're more likely to be approved for mortgages, car loans, and other types of credit when needed.
- **Better rental options**: Many landlords check credit scores when evaluating potential tenants, so having good credit can help you qualify for better rental properties.
- **Lower insurance premiums**: Some insurance companies use credit scores to determine premiums, so having good credit could lead to lower rates on car insurance, homeowners' insurance, and other types of coverage.
- **More negotiating power**: With good credit, you may negotiate better terms on loans, credit cards, and other financial products.

To build and maintain good credit, you must use credit facilities, like credit cards, loans, and accounts, responsibly, on time, and consistently. What this means is:

- Paying your bills before their due date.
- Keeping your balances low.
- Not using too much credit at one time.
- Take the time to check your credit report for errors or any signs of identity theft—you'll learn how to do this later.

On the flip side, bad credit is like waving around a giant financial red flag that can make it harder to borrow money, qualify for loans, and even get a job or an apartment. When you have bad credit, lenders and creditors see you as a higher-risk borrower. This can lead to higher interest rates, lower credit limits, or not getting credit at all!

When you have bad credit, you'll end up:

- **paying higher interest rates**: When you have bad credit, lenders may charge you higher interest rates on loans and credit cards to offset the perceived risk of lending to you.
- **find it difficult to be approved for credit**: With bad credit, you may be denied mortgages, car loans, credit cards, and other types of credit, or you may only qualify for expensive loans.
- **having limited rental options**: Many landlords check credit scores when screening potential tenants, so having bad credit could make it harder to qualify for certain rental properties.
- **have higher insurance premiums**: Some insurance companies use credit scores to determine premiums, so having bad credit could lead to higher rates on car insurance, homeowners' insurance, and other types of coverage.
- **finding it difficult to get a job**: Some employers check credit reports as part of the hiring process, especially for positions that involve handling money or sensitive information.

So, what causes bad credit? There are a few common culprits when it comes to bad credit. These are:

- Late or missed payments on bills and loans.
- High credit card balances or maxed-out credit cards.
- Defaulting on loans or declaring bankruptcy.
- Having too many credit inquiries in a short time.
- Errors or fraudulent activity on your credit report.

Bad credit isn't the end of the world, though! The steps you can take to improve your credit are listed below.

Escape the Debt Trap: Proven Strategies for a Debt-Free Life

Debt is a word that adults often throw around, but it is rarely explained. In its simplest form, debt is money you borrow from a lender, with the promise to pay it back over time, usually with interest. Common forms of debt for teens include personal and student loans and credit cards. While debt can be scary, it can also be a powerful tool for achieving your financial goals. So, how can debt be good or bad? Let's break it down.

Good debt can help you build wealth or achieve important life goals over time. Some examples of good debt can include properly managed student loans, mortgages, or business loans. Good debt is money you use wisely, with a clear plan for how to use it and pay it back.

Bad debt, on the other hand, is debt that doesn't provide long-term benefits and can actually harm financial health over time. Some examples of bad debt include poorly managed credit cards, revolving loans, payday loans, and luxury car loans.

The problem with bad debt is that it often comes with high interest rates and fees and doesn't provide any long-term value. In fact, bad debt can actually hold you back from achieving your financial goals! All debt is not made equal, but all debt must be used and paid back responsibly.

Common Causes of Uncontrolled Debt

Now, you know that debt can be a valuable tool for achieving your financial goals, but when it spirals out of control, it can quickly become a major source of stress. You'll need to understand how people end up in a debt trap so that you can avoid making the same mistakes and make smart choices about borrowing and managing your money.

- **Low income**: When you're not earning enough money to cover your basic expenses, it can be tempting to turn to debt to make ends meet. This can quickly turn into a vicious cycle, where you're borrowing more and more money just to keep up with your bills.
- **Medical bills**: Unexpected medical expenses can be a significant source of debt, especially if you don't have proper health insurance coverage or medical savings.
- **Job loss**: Losing your job can be a major financial setback, especially if you don't have an emergency fund to fall back on. Without a steady income, it can be difficult to keep up with your bills and avoid falling into debt.
- **Poorly managed student loans**: College education costs have skyrocketed, leaving many students with significant debt burdens after graduation. While student loans can be a form of good debt if they lead to higher earning potential, they can also be a major source of financial stress if not managed carefully.
- **Car loans and mortgages**: Taking on a car loan or mortgage can be a smart financial move, but it's important to borrow wisely and make sure you can afford the monthly payments. If you borrow more than you can realistically afford, you may struggle to keep up with your bills and fall behind on your payments.
- **Credit cards**: Credit cards can be convenient ways to make purchases and build credit, but they can also be a major source of uncontrolled debt. High interest rates and fees can make it difficult to pay off balances.

- **Payday, title, and cash loans**: These short-term loans can be tempting when you're in a financial bind, but they often come with sky-high interest rates and fees that can trap you in a cycle of debt. It's best to avoid these types of loans altogether!
- **Poor money management**: Living beyond your means, failing to budget, and not saving for emergencies can all contribute to uncontrolled debt. It's important to have a clear understanding of your income and expenses and to make a plan for managing your money wisely.
- **Unexpected emergencies**: Life is full of surprises, and sometimes those surprises come with a hefty price tag. These could be unexpected car or home repairs, medical emergencies, or unexpected expenses.
- **High costs of living**: Living in an area with a high cost of living can make it challenging to keep up with expenses, even if you're earning a decent income. If you struggle to afford basic necessities like housing, food, and transportation, you may turn to debt to fill the gaps.

Remember, uncontrolled debt can happen to anyone, but it doesn't have to define your financial future. You can control your debt by being proactive and making intelligent choices about borrowing and managing your money!

How to Avoid Falling Into Debt

As I mentioned before, debt can be a powerful tool for achieving your goals, but it can also be a slippery slope to financial trouble if not managed carefully. To avoid falling into debt traps, you must be proactive and strategic about your money management. Here are some key tips to keep in mind:

- **Budgeting**: Creating and sticking to a budget is one of the most powerful ways to avoid overspending and falling into debt.
- **Avoid overspending**: One of the teens' biggest mistakes with debt is overspending. To avoid this trap, be mindful of your spending habits and make sure you're living within your means. Remember your minimum monthly payment and remind yourself that credit is limited.
- **Have an emergency fund**: Building an emergency fund is crucial for avoiding debt when unexpected expenses arise. Aim to save up at least six months' worth of living expenses in a separate savings account you can tap into when needed.
- **Pay off credit card balances**: Credit card debt can be one of the most dangerous types of debt, thanks to high interest rates and fees. The best way to avoid falling into this trap is only to spend what you can pay back in one installment.
- **Avoid unnecessary expenses**: Review your spending habits closely and identify any expenses you can reduce or eliminate.
- **Avoid cash advances**: Cash advances from credit cards or payday loans can be tempting when you're short on cash. However, they often come with sky-high interest rates and fees that can quickly spiral out of control. .

Apps and Tools to Manage Debt

Managing debt can feel overwhelming, but being a modern teen means you have many apps and tools available to help you manage your debt more efficiently. Make sure you download only verified apps. Here are some of my top recommendations.

- Debt Payoff Planner: The Debt Payoff Planner is a simple and effective tool for creating a personalized debt repayment plan. It is excellent if you want a straightforward and customizable approach to debt repayment.
- Bright Money: This app uses artificial intelligence to optimize your debt repayment and savings. It is a good option if you want a hands-off approach to debt management and are comfortable with automation.
- Qapital: This app helps you save money and pay off debt through gamification and goal-setting. Qapital is a good choice if you need help saving money and want a fun and engaging approach to debt management.
- Trim: Trim is an app that helps you save money and negotiate bills to free up more money for debt repayment. It is a good option to save money on bills and subscriptions without much effort.
- Undebt.it: This is a web-based tool for creating and tracking your debt repayment plan. Undebt.it is a good option if you want a simple and customizable approach to debt repayment and prefer a web-based tool.

How Well Do You Understand Credit Lingo Exercise

This exercise is the same as your first exercise in Chapter 1. This time, however, you'll be given a list of standard credit terms. Try to match each term with the corresponding word. Assign the word or phrase's number next to the definitions provided in the table below.

Term	Number
A payment option that gives you the ability to buy something now with somebody else's money.	
A card issued by a lender that gives the cardholder the ability to borrow money in advance.	
The maximum amount of money you can borrow on a credit card.	
A credit card that allows you withdraw cash from an ATM or financial institution. The interest is often higher than with other credit card transactions.	
A person that takes out a loan with a promise to pay it back later with interest.	
The initial amount of money borrowed.	

1. Credit card
2. Capital
3. Borrower
4. Credit
5. Credit limit
6. Cash advance

With knowledge of credit and debt, you can begin building an excellent credit score and setting yourself up for success. Remember, debt should be used responsibly and with a goal in mind. If you've already fallen into debt, please don't panic! The strategies in this chapter will help you fix your mistakes. Once you've mastered these strategies, it's time to level up and start building future wealth.

CHAPTER 7

INVEST FOR SUCCESS:

THE TEEN'S PLAYBOOK FOR WEALTH CREATION

L earning about investing and the different investment options available to you might feel intimidating at first, but trust me; it's one of the most powerful tools you have for building long-term wealth and financial security. An easy way to think about investing is putting your money into something with the expectation that it will grow in value over time and generate returns for you.

While traditional savings accounts are safe, they don't earn much interest, and if you want to build real wealth, you need to maximize the bang for your buck. That is where investing comes in—it's a tool to help your money grow over time. The key to investing is to choose the right investments and to start early. You must also invest consistently, dedicating your savings to specific investment options after a certain time. Here are the best options to consider.

Stocks

Stocks are one of the most common and popular investment types. However, they can be a bit confusing for beginners, so let's break it down in simple terms.

When you buy a stock, you're buying a small piece of ownership in a company—think of it like becoming a part-owner of a company, even if your ownership stake is small. Being a part owner means you now have a claim on a portion of the company's assets and earnings. If the company you bought stocks in does well and makes a profit, the value of your stock may go up, and you could sell it for more than you paid for it, making a profit. Conversely, if the company performs poorly, the value of your stock may go down, and you could lose money if you sell it for less than you paid.

One important thing to understand about stocks is that they experience fluctuations according to what the economic market is doing. Because of this, the stock market can be volatile, which means your investment risk is higher. When investing in stocks, there are a few key things to remember:

- You will need to have a variety of stocks across different industries and sectors. This spreading of your risk is called diversifying your portfolio.
- Before investing in a company, you will need to do proper research.
- Stocks are best suited for long-term investing, so you must be patient and ignore short-term price fluctuations.
- Start small with your stock investments and put only some of your savings into stocks.

Bonds

Bonds are financial investment facilities that allow you to lend money to a company or government. Just like when you have to pay interest on the money you have borrowed, the company or government needs to pay back what you loaned them with interest after a certain amount of time has passed.

Interest rates on bonds are known as coupon rates, and they're fixed for the entire life of the bond. Investing in bonds is a great way to know exactly how much money you will get back from your investment.

There are different types of bonds you can invest in, and they include:

- **Corporate Bonds**: Issued by companies to raise money for various projects or expenses.
- **Municipal Bonds**: Issued by states, cities, or other local governments to fund public projects like building schools or highways.
- **Treasury Bonds**: Issued by the federal government to finance government spending.

Before you invest in bonds, you must consider the issuer's credit-worthiness, coupon rate, and maturity dates.

Mutual Funds

Mutual funds are quite popular for teens because they allow you to combine your money with other investors to buy a collection of stocks, bonds, or other securities. It's like joining a big investment club where everyone puts their money together to make more money!

When you invest in a mutual fund, you're buying shares of the fund, not individual stocks or bonds. This fund is managed by a professional who decides where to invest everyone's money and buys and sells based on the fund's goals.

The biggest perk of investing in mutual funds is instant diversification. With a single investment, you can own a small piece of hundreds or even thousands of different investment options. A diverse investment portfolio reduces the risk of investing. In addition, you don't need to do any of the guesswork because your fund manager will do all the hard work.

No investment comes without a downside, though. Regarding mutual funds, you may be charged annual fees and the potential for your investment not to make much money. To reduce the risk of not making money, take the time to research your fund, its goals, any fees, and how it performed in the past.

Real Estate

Real estate might not sound like an investment—but it is! However, you need to pay to maintain the properties you own. For most teens, investing in real estate investment trusts (REITs) is a better option than owning physical property. These are companies that own and manage different income-generating properties, and you can buy a small piece of their real estate portfolio.

Like mutual funds, a professional portfolio manager will do all the work for you, and most portfolios have a bunch of different property types, like apartment and office buildings, shopping malls, and warehouses. Some REITs even generate income from cell phone towers!

You need to know that there are two main REIT types—equity and mortgage. Equity REITs own and manage physical properties, and mortgage REITs invest in mortgage-backed assets that get income from the interest charged on other people's mortgages.

Savings Bonds

Our final teen-friendly investment option is savings bonds. This is a loan that the government takes from you. In return, the government promises to pay back your loaned amount with interest. Now, savings bonds shouldn't be confused with the bonds we chatted about above. While they're similar, savings bonds are 100% government-funded, which means they're way more secure.

Savings bonds come in two types: Series EE bonds, which have fixed interest for up to 30 years, and Series I bonds, which combine fixed interest with inflation rates that are adjusted twice a year. The best part of savings bonds is that they're very affordable. You can start investing for just $25, and if you hold onto your savings bond for at least five years, you won't owe any tax on the interest you earn.

Why Start Early?

OK, so saving and investing early on might not sound like a whole lot of fun at the moment, but here's the thing—it has the potential to accelerate your financial freedom and independence. Starting early has many advantages, so let's discuss some pros.

1. **Time**: When you start saving and investing early, you have the power of time. This means even small amounts of money can grow into considerable sums over time, thanks to the magic of compound interest.
2. **Learning opportunity**: Nobody expects you to be perfect because no human being is, but being young means that you can learn from your mistakes early without risking all your savings. You can find out what savings accounts and investment options work best for you.
3. **Higher risk tolerance**: Another significant advantage of investing early is that you can take more risks. While this means you may lose some money in the short term, you can recover much quicker in the long run.
4. **Developing positive financial habits**: Starting to save early is also a great way to work out your financial habit muscles.

When you prioritize saving from a young age, it becomes a natural part of your financial routine, and these habits can pay off big time down the road.

5. **Long-term wealth building**: One of the most enormous benefits of saving early is the potential for long-term wealth building. When you give your money time to grow, you can build a significant nest egg throughout your career.

6. **Less pressure on income**: If you wait until you're older to start saving, you may have to play catch-up and save a much larger percentage of your income to reach your goals. But if you start early and let your money grow over time, you can achieve your goals with a smaller percentage of your income.

7. **Financial goals and dreams**: Starting to save early can also help you achieve your financial goals and dreams. Whether you want to buy a house, travel the world, or start your own business, having a solid savings foundation can make those dreams a reality.

As you can see, early savings and investment habits can make a big difference in the years to come. From retiring early to enjoying life by fulfilling your needs and wants, starting early is anything but boring. So, start small, be consistent, and watch your savings grow over time.

The Power of Growth: Grasping the Power of Compound Interest

It's time to let you in on a secret and one of the most powerful financial forces in the world—compounding! Trust me when I say, understanding how compound interest works can totally transform your financial future.

So why is compound interest so powerful? There are a few key reasons.

- It accounts for time so that your money can grow safely.
- Compounding is powerful for teens because you have time on your side.
- Even small savings can make a big difference when you're younger; as you get older, you can contribute more to earn more.
- Compounding works for you 24/7, 365 days a year, and you don't have to do anything other than invest your money.

Of course, there are a couple of things to keep in mind. First, compound interest only works if you let your money stay invested. If you constantly withdraw your earnings, you'll miss out on the power of compounding. Second, compound interest isn't all magic —you must invest consistently and choose investments that offer a good potential return.

Smart Money Moves: Exploring Safe Investment Options

So, there's one more super important topic we need to discuss regarding investment: risk and return. Let's begin with return. When you invest your money, the goal is to make more money, right? That extra money you make is called your return. Risk is the money you are investing.

Generally, investments with higher risk also have the potential for higher returns. For example, investing in a brand-new company that has yet to make any money is usually riskier than investing in a big, established company that's been around for decades. The newer company might have a higher potential return, but it also has a higher chance of failing and losing your money.

On the other hand, some investments are considered pretty safe, like government bonds. The return on government bonds is usually pretty low, but the risk is also very low—there's almost no chance that the government will fail to pay you back.

As an investor, your job is to find the right balance of risk and return for your goals and comfort level. You're young and have a lot of time to ride out the ups and downs of the market, so you might be willing to take on more risk in exchange for the potential of higher returns.

What Is Risk Tolerance?

One way to think about risk tolerance is to imagine your investments as a rollercoaster. If you have a high-risk tolerance, you might be the person who runs straight for the biggest, loopiest coaster in the park. If you have a low-risk tolerance, you might prefer the kiddie coaster or the merry-go-round. And if you have a moderate risk tolerance, you might go for the coaster that's somewhere in between—thrilling but not too scary. The key is to be honest with yourself about how much risk you're really comfortable with. It's okay to adjust your risk tolerance over time as your goals and circumstances change.

Remember, investing always involves some risk. Even the safest investments can lose money if the economy takes a nosedive. You need to find the right balance of risk and return and diversify your investments so you're not putting all your eggs in one basket.

Still, you shouldn't let risk scare you away, risk is sometimes a good thing! Without risk, there would be no reward—you just need to find the middle ground between risk and return. With everything you know about these types of investment options, you should be confident in your ability to overcome any risks associated with each option.

The Basics of Cryptocurrency

First things first—don't let anyone convince you that cryptocurrency is low risk because it's not. In fact, it's very volatile, which means it comes with high risk but the potential for high reward as well. With that disclaimer out of the way, let's dive in!

Cryptocurrency is a digital or virtual currency that uses cryptography—a fancy word for secret codes—to secure and verify transactions. Unlike traditional money, which is issued and regulated by governments, cryptocurrency operates on decentralized networks, which means no single authority controls it.

The Types of Cryptocurrencies

As of 2023, there are over 10,000 different cryptocurrencies in existence, each with its own unique features, purpose, and value proposition. While it would be impossible to cover them all, let's look at some of the most popular and well-known cryptocurrencies you might encounter.

- **Bitcoin (BTC)**: Bitcoin is the OG of cryptocurrencies, the one that started it all. Created in 2009 by the mysterious Satoshi Nakamoto, Bitcoin is a decentralized digital currency that can be sent and received without a central authority like a bank. It's the largest and most valuable cryptocurrency by market cap and is often used as a store of value or a hedge against inflation.
- **Ethereum (ETH)**: Ethereum is more than just a cryptocurrency; it's a decentralized platform for building and running smart contracts and decentralized applications (dApps). Ether, the native currency of the Ethereum network, is used to pay for transaction fees and computational services. Ethereum has created a wide range

of decentralized finance (DeFi) applications, from lending and borrowing platforms to prediction markets and asset management tools.

- **Tether (USDT)**: Tether is a stablecoin, meaning its value is pegged to the value of a traditional currency like the US dollar. Each Tether token is supposed to be backed by one US dollar held in reserve, making it a popular choice for traders who want to move money between different cryptocurrencies without exposing themselves to the market's volatility. However, Tether has been controversial because people have asked whether it actually holds enough reserves to back all of its tokens.

- **Dogecoin (DOGE)**: Believe it or not, Dogecoin started as a joke, a meme coin based on the popular "Doge" internet meme featuring a Shiba Inu dog. However, it quickly gained a following and became a legitimate cryptocurrency with a loyal community of supporters. While it doesn't have any unique technical features or use cases, Dogecoin has been used to tip content creators online. Celebrities like Elon Musk have promoted it.

- **Solana (SOL)**: This high-performance blockchain platform is designed for fast, cheap, scalable decentralized applications (dApps). It uses a unique combination of proof-of-stake and proof-of-history consensus mechanisms and a novel approach to parallel transaction processing to achieve transaction speeds of up to 65,000 per second. Solana's native currency is SOL.

- **Litecoin (LTC)**: Litecoin is one of the oldest and most well-established cryptocurrencies. It's sometimes called the "silver to Bitcoin's gold." Litecoin was created in 2011 as a faster, cheaper, and more scalable alternative to Bitcoin, with a larger supply and a different mining algorithm. It has a strong community of supporters and is widely accepted by merchants and exchanges.

Crypto comes with higher risks. That said, the higher the risk, the higher the potential for reward, and if you have a higher tolerance for investment risks, you may consider putting a small amount into crypto.

Growing Your Money Through Retirement Savings: Roth IRA and 401K Accounts

Let's first define a Roth IRA. IRA stands for Individual Retirement Account, and a Roth IRA is a specific type of IRA with unique tax benefits. With a Roth IRA, you contribute money that you've already paid taxes on—like money from your summer job or allowance—and you can then invest that money in different assets like stocks, bonds, or mutual funds.

Now, how does a Roth IRA compare to other types of retirement accounts, like a 401(k)? The main difference is that a 401(k) is an employer-sponsored retirement plan, whereas a Roth IRA is an individual account that you open and manage on your own. With a 401(k), your contributions are typically made with pre-tax dollars, which means you don't pay taxes on the money you put in, but you do pay taxes when you withdraw the money in retirement. Some employers also offer a Roth 401(k) option, which works similarly to a Roth IRA but with higher contribution limits.

So, why should teenagers consider investing in a Roth IRA? The main reason is the power of compound growth over time. The earlier you start investing, the more time your money has to grow and compound. Let's say you start investing $100 monthly in a Roth IRA when you're 18 years old, earning an average annual return of 7%. By age 65, that account could be worth over $500,000 —all from just a small monthly contribution over time.

The Pros and Cons of Roth IRAs and 401ks

When it comes to saving for retirement, two of the most popular options are Roth IRAs and 401(k)s. Both of these accounts offer tax benefits and the potential for long-term growth. Still, they also have some key differences that are important to understand.

Roth IRA Pros

- **Tax-free growth and withdrawals in retirement**: As discussed earlier, one of the most significant advantages of a Roth IRA is that your investments can grow tax-free over time, and you won't have to pay taxes on your withdrawals in retirement—assuming you follow the rules.
- **Flexibility**: With a Roth IRA, you have much control over your investments. You can choose from a wide range of options, including stocks, bonds, mutual funds, and more. You can also withdraw your original contributions at any time without penalty.
- **No required minimum distributions (RMDs)**: Unlike traditional IRAs and 401(k)s, Roth IRAs don't have required minimum distributions (RMDs). That means you can let your money continue to grow tax-free for as long as you want.

Roth IRA Cons

- **Income limits**: Not everyone is eligible to contribute to a Roth IRA. Suppose your income is above a certain level. In that case, you may be limited in how much you can contribute or not allowed to contribute at all.

- **Lower contribution limits**: Compared to a 401(k), Roth IRAs have lower annual contribution limits. For 2024, the maximum contribution is $7,000—$8,000 if you're 50 or older.
- **No employer match**: Unlike some 401(k)s, Roth IRAs don't come with an employer match. That means you're on your own when funding the account.

401(k) Pros

- **Higher contribution limits**: 401(k)s have much higher annual contribution limits than Roth IRAs. For 2024, you can contribute up to $23,000—$30,500 if you're 50 or older.
- **Employer match**: Many employers offer a matching contribution to their employees' 401(k)s. This is essentially free money that can help supercharge your retirement savings.
- **Automatic contributions**: With a 401(k), your contributions are typically deducted automatically from your paycheck, making it easy to save consistently over time.

401(k) Cons

- **Limited investment options**: Compared to a Roth IRA, 401(k)s typically have a more limited selection of investment options. You're usually restricted to the funds offered by your employer's plan.
- **Potential fees**: Some 401(k) plans have high fees that can reduce investment returns over time. It's important to understand your plan's fees and how they compare to other options.

- **Early withdrawal penalties**: If you need to withdraw money from your 401(k) before age 59 1/2, you may face a 10% early withdrawal penalty in addition to ordinary income taxes.

So, which is better? The truth is, there's no one-size-fits-all answer. Your best option will depend on your financial situation, goals, and eligibility. If you're eligible for a Roth IRA and like the idea of tax-free growth and flexibility, it can be a great option—especially if you're just starting out and in a lower tax bracket.

On the other hand, if you have access to a 401(k) with a generous employer match, it may make sense to prioritize that account to take advantage of the free money. Ideally, if you have the means, it can be an intelligent move to contribute to both a Roth IRA and a 401(k). That way, you can take advantage of the unique benefits of each account.

Getting Started in the Investment World: Investing in Stocks

Investing in the stock market can be a great way to grow your wealth over time and build a secure financial future. But if you're new to investing, it can feel overwhelming and intimidating. You'll need to know where to get started with trading stocks to make money and build future wealth.

- **Define your investment goals**: Before you start investing, it's important to have a clear idea of what you're trying to achieve. Your investment goals will help guide your decisions about what types of stocks to invest in.
- **Assess your risk tolerance**: It's vital to assess your risk tolerance. If the thought of losing money makes you queasy, you may want to stick with more conservative investments.

- **Choose an investment account**: To start investing in stocks, you must open an investment account. Brokerage accounts are general-purpose accounts that allow you to buy and sell stocks, bonds, and other securities.
- **Decide on an investment strategy**: There are many different approaches to investing in stocks, and no one strategy is right for everyone.
- **Set a budget**: Before buying stocks, you'll have to budget for how much you can afford to invest. A good rule of thumb is only to invest money you won't need for at least 5 years since the stock market can be volatile in the short term.
- **Select your investments**: Once you've opened an account and decided on a strategy, it's time to start picking stocks! This can be the most exciting—and nerve-wracking, part of the process. You'll need to do your research, looking for companies with solid financials, competitive advantages, and growth potential. If you're uncomfortable picking individual stocks, consider investing in a diversified fund that tracks a market index.
- **Diversify your portfolio**: Diversification is critical to managing risk in your stock portfolio. In addition to diversifying across different companies and sectors, consider other asset classes like bonds, real estate, or commodities. The goal is to create a well-rounded portfolio that can weather different market conditions.
- **Monitor and rebalance your portfolio**: It's essential to regularly monitor your investments and make adjustments as needed. This might include selling stocks that have become overvalued, buying new stocks that meet your criteria, or rebalancing your portfolio to maintain your desired asset allocation.

Your Investment Profile Questionnaire

To figure out your investment risk profile and the best options for you when it comes to investing, you will need some guidance. Fill in the questionnaire below so that you can use it to assess what your investment needs are when chatting with a broker or the adult helping you invest.

1. My goals for investing are?
2. What is my attitude when it comes to investing? Am I fearful, somewhere in between, confident?
3. When do I plan on withdrawing my investments?
4. How many years do I want to withdraw?
5. Do I feel a need to protect my investments and savings at all costs?
6. When I think about investing, do I mind some risk, and how much?
7. What is my next big-ticket purchase?
8. What do I expect my income to be in the next 5 years?
9. What kinds of stock options most interest me?
10. If I had a lot of money, what would be the first investment option I'd invest in?

While all of the information you've just learned is important, some might resonate more with you than others. I encourage you to take the time to write down the options that interest you and do some extra research. Investment is an excellent start to your financial future. Still, you'll also need to know how to overcome challenges when they arise, and that's what you'll learn next.

CHAPTER 8

READY, SET, ADAPT:

TACKLING FINANCIAL CURVEBALLS
LIKE A PRO

B efore you begin with this section, I need to get real with you —at some point in your life, you will face financial challenges. Thankfully, when you're younger, these challenges are rarely catastrophic. By knowing what they are, you can better equip yourself to avoid them or recover much more quickly. These common challenges include:

- Not earning enough money
- Spending more than you earn
- Borrowing money from friends or paying for friends
- Struggling to meet savings goals
- Unhealthy financial relationships
- Job-related issues

Always remember that financial challenges are a normal part of life, but they don't have to derail your financial goals. Try to stay ahead of and aware of common hurdles and take proactive steps to overcome them. This way, you can stay on track and build a strong financial foundation for your future.

Dealing With the Ups and Downs of Income

With a bit of planning, a splash of discipline, and some adaptability skills, you can learn to ride the waves of financial ups and downs like a pro. Here are some steps for staying afloat no matter what life throws your way.

- Define your essential monthly expenses
- Track your spending carefully
- Estimate your lowest monthly income
- Identify non-essential expenses
- Create your new monthly budget
- **Pro tip:** If you have variable income, it can be helpful to think about your finances on a month-to-month basis rather than an annual one. Divide your annual income by 12 to get an average monthly amount and use that as a starting point for your budget.

Remember that variable income is not usually a permanent fixture in your life. Things will get better, so make sure you keep your budget accessible and that you can adjust it according to your current circumstances. The temporary nature of financial ups and downs also means you need to remain disciplined regarding your money. Stay focused on your goals, choose to save for the stuff you really want, and keep your cash safe and secure for your future.

Finally, always remember that some months will be more expensive than others. Holidays, birthdays, and back-to-school shopping can quickly bust your budget if you don't plan accordingly for them. When possible, set some money aside each month to cover any extra costs you know are coming.

How to Boost Your Income Temporarily

So, you've examined your finances and your debt, and you've realized that you need to boost your income to get through this tough financial downturn.

First things first: Hold on, teen. It won't last forever. Second, living in a modern world means you have plenty of opportunities to increase your cash flow, dig yourself out of debt, or even afford to go on a vacation with your friends without having to dip into your savings.

- **Start a side hustle**: This could be anything from tutoring or pet-sitting to selling handmade crafts or offering your skills as a freelancer. Think about what you're good at and what people in your community might need, and then get creative!
- **Take on odd jobs**: This could include mowing lawns, walking dogs, shoveling snow, or helping neighbors with household tasks.
- **Sell stuff you no longer need**: We all have stuff lying around that we no longer use or need. Host a yard sale, list items on online marketplaces like eBay or Facebook Marketplace, or take them to a consignment shop.
- **Participate in paid surveys or focus groups**: Did you know you can get paid for your opinions? There are tons of companies out there that will pay you to take surveys, test products, or participate in focus groups.
- **Taking extra shifts**: If you already have a part-time job, one of the easiest ways to boost your income is to take on extra shifts when they're available. Of course, you'll want to ensure that extra shifts don't interfere with your schoolwork or other commitments.

- **Seasonal work**: This work can be done when you're not busy, like summer break or the holidays.

Emergency Funds to Keep Your Cash Safe

One thing a lot of teens overlook is an emergency fund. This small but powerful financial tool can swoop in and save the day. You need an emergency fund because when things go wrong, it can really put a damper on other areas of your life. Instead of dipping into savings and investments for sudden expenses, an emergency fund can help you get by without having to borrow money or forgo your dreams.

Building an emergency savings fund might not sound like a super exciting financial goal, but it is one of the most important things you will ever do to secure your money and ensure that life's ups and downs don't derail you altogether. Don't think of the larger amount now; put aside a little bit every month, and over time, you will begin to accumulate more than enough cash to see you through in emergency situations.

Building Resilience in Financial Matters

The twists and turns we've been chatting about can be challenging. Still, there's one more amazing skill you can use to weather financial storms—resilience! Building resilience is incredible because it provides you with the strength and tenacity to face any challenge that comes your way, with the belief that you can bounce back stronger than ever. Financial resilience can be broken down into two key aspects, so let's look at what they are.

- **Setting realistic expectations**: You must set realistic expectations for your finances. There's no point in having a goal of putting away $3,000 toward savings every month if you have no way of doing this. You can't expect to become a millionaire overnight or never face a financial setback. You must stay focused on steadily progressing toward your goals, one step at a time. Success is very rarely a straight line. You will have ups and downs and twists and turns along the way.

- **Patience, persistence, and perseverance**: Once you've become honest about your finances, you can work on your patience and commitment to your goals. Remember, you need to be able to turn your FOMO to JOMO and think of your money habits as building muscle–the more you work at it, the stronger and more resilient you become. Every time you face a financial challenge and come out the other side, you're building the skills and confidence you need to tackle even bigger obstacles in the future.

Building financial resilience will increase your chances of a comfortable retirement because you have a solid financial foundation that you've built over time. You will also have solid emergency funds to handle your debt better and easily handle unplanned costs. You can begin to use debt to your advantage and get rid of that high-interest, bad debt that is holding you back from your financial destiny. Slowly but surely, you'll improve your lifestyle as you build your good money habits.

Of course, like all other good things in life, financial resilience takes time, effort, and a willingness to batten down the hatches and stay the course when things get a little challenging. But if you're realistic, patient, and persistent, you'll realize that no storm lasts forever and that your financial journey can still be a successful one—just keep your eyes on the prize, teen!

Keeping Your Finances Safe

While the convenience of banking and investing online is an advantage for most modern teens, you also need to be extra careful with your online information. Cybercriminals are really sneaky, tricking you into providing them with your valuable financial info. Don't worry, though; with a few simple tips and tricks, you can become a master of securing your financial cybersecurity so that your information is locked down tighter than Fort Knox.

- Use strong passwords
- Update your systems and software
- Just delete suspicious emails
- Invest in security software
- Shred your statements
- Lock your electronic devices

Staying cyber-safe might seem like a drag, but it can save you from a lot of heartbreak and frustration. Stay vigilant, perhaps a little paranoid, and keep your money safe!

You might be wondering, what can happen if my information gets hacked or unsavory people get hold of it? Well, here's the thing: it's not just about losing your money; you could temporarily lose your identity, too, and that's a huge deal! Identity theft can result in:

- Financial loss
- Credit damage
- Legal issues
- Emotional distress

Identity theft is a serious threat that can have devastating consequences for your financial, legal, and emotional well-being. But by taking proactive steps to protect your personal information, like using strong passwords and choosing secure financial tools, you can reduce your risk and stay one step ahead of the bad guys.

Creating a Recovery Plan

You may have already fallen victim to identity theft, or you could have made one of the common mistakes teens make, and now you're in some financial trouble. The good news is that you're young, which means you have time on your side when it comes to recovering from financial setbacks.

First, you'll want to remain calm and accept your situation. As much as you would love a time machine right now, it's not a realistic request, so you'll need to create a financial recovery plan to get back on your feet–let's take a look at how.

Step 1: Take Inventory

The first step in any good recovery plan is to take an honest look at your current situation. It's like taking a financial selfie; you might not like what you see at first, but it's imperative to have a clear picture of where you're starting from.

- What are your remaining assets?
- How much money do you owe?
- How much income do you bring in each month?
- How much do you spend?
- What is your credit score?

Step 2: Negotiating Payment Plans

Once you have a clear picture of your financial situation, it's time to start tackling those debts. One option is to contact your creditors and see if you can negotiate a payment plan. This means working out a schedule to pay off your debts over time rather than all at once. When negotiating a payment plan, be honest about your situation and what you can realistically afford to pay each month. Many creditors will work with you, especially if you're proactive about finding a solution.

You can also look into debt consolidation or credit counseling services, which can help you combine your debts into one manageable payment or develop a plan to pay them off over time. Recovering from a financial setback is never easy, but it is possible. Take stock of your situation, create a budget, and explore your options for repayment to start digging yourself out of the hole and build a brighter financial future.

Step 3: Recovering Your Credit Score

Let's begin by talking about what your credit score is. This three-digit number lets lenders know whether you're good at borrowing money and paying it back. The higher your score, the more trustworthy potential lenders perceive you to be.

If your credit score has taken a hit, you may be feeling a couple of pretty negative things, and you may even believe that your financial future is bleak. But the cool thing about a credit score is that it's like a phoenix, and with enough coaxing and some clever strategies, you can have your financial future rising from the ashes!

Now, here's the good news: building your credit score is the same as rebuilding it! So get to rebuilding, and when things feel too difficult, remember that a good score can open doors to better loan rates, higher credit limits, and even job opportunities down the road. Keep in mind your credit score doesn't define you. Everyone makes mistakes; what's important is that you learn from them. To learn from your mistakes and setbacks, you need to reframe what has happened. Instead of looking at your mistakes as a big problem that cannot be overcome, think of them as problems that can be solved. Because, let's face it, with some creativity, experimentation, and brainstorming, just about every problem can be solved.

Learning From Setbacks

We've been talking a lot about the nitty-gritty details of recovering from financial setbacks. Still, I want to take a moment to focus on something just as important—your mindset. It's easy to get bogged down in negative thoughts when facing a financial challenge. You might feel like you've failed or will never be able to bounce back. Wrong! Every setback is an opportunity for growth and learning. It's all about how you choose to look at it. Having a positive, growth-oriented mindset allows you to open yourself up to a world of possibilities regarding your finances.

You've learned what it takes to dodge financial curveballs like a pro and how to get back up if and when you fall. Now, it's time to begin paving your pathway to financial independence and future wealth. So, grab your notebook, and let's get to your final chapter—the key to unlocking a financially healthier you!

CHAPTER 9

FUTUREPROOF FINANCE:

PAVING YOUR PATH TO FINANCIAL INDEPENDENCE

M any people have the ultimate goal of becoming financially independent. Still, some of them need to learn what this means! In its simplest form, financial independence is when you have enough income from your investments, savings, and other passive income sources to support your lifestyle without needing to work a traditional 9-to-5 job—ah, an absolute dream!

Now, before you throw your hands in the air and say that's impossible, all of the work you've done in reading this book and completing your exercises has set you up so that it is possible. The goal is to have your money working for you 24-7 and to have that money continue to grow no matter what you're doing with your time.

Aside from the obvious advantages of not having to work and your money growing without much effort, financial independence comes with these other benefits:

- Greater control over your life
- Learning the value of money
- Building and protecting your credit score
- Saving money
- Developing career skills
- Greater financial security
- Freedom of choice
- Building confidence
- Peace of mind

Many people want financial independence. Still, some really want to work and enjoy their careers. The reality is at some point, everyone has to stop working. I know that is far off for you, but it's important to start thinking about what age you want to reach this financial achievement.

Road to Riches: Your Adventure Towards Financial Independence

After reading all of the info in this book, you're convinced and ready to take control of your money and start building the life of your dreams. Great! You'll need to know what steps must be taken to achieve financial independence. Let's look at these before getting into some of the nitty-gritty of futureproofing your finances.

- **Get good grades**: Getting good grades opens up opportunities for scholarships, grants, and higher-paying jobs down the road. It's an investment in your future earning potential, so hit those books!
- **Develop uncommon skills**: Consider learning a second language, picking up a musical instrument, or mastering a specialized software program. The more you can differentiate yourself from the crowd, the more valuable you'll be to potential employers or clients.

- **Develop good habits**: Start developing good money habits early, like tracking your spending, saving a portion of every paycheck, and avoiding unnecessary debt. The earlier you start, the easier it will be to maintain those habits for life.
- **Get a job**: Not only will you earn some cash, but you'll also gain valuable work experience and start building your professional network.
- **Start a side hustle**: Try to find something you enjoy doing that also has the potential to generate some extra cash.
- **Invest in yourself**: This could mean taking a course to learn a new skill, attending a conference to network with others in your field, or even starting your own business.
- **Use credit wisely**: Start building a solid credit score early, as this will open up opportunities for better loan rates and higher credit limits in the future.
- **Build a network**: Attend industry events, join professional organizations, and seek opportunities to connect with others who share your goals and values. You never know when a casual connection might lead to a life-changing opportunity.

Remember, achieving financial independence is a marathon, not a sprint. It takes time, effort, and a willingness to keep learning and growing. But if you start taking these steps today, you'll be well on your way to building the financial future of your dreams.

Establish Your Definition of Financial Independence

To work toward your definition of financial independence, you must have conversations about your financial goals. If you and your parents are tight, ask them for guidance and what mistakes they made when beginning their financial journey. Even if you don't want advice, discussing your financial goals and what you're working towards can mean you always have the best cheerleaders in your corner.

You'll need to figure out what financial independence and success actually mean to you. There is no one-size-fits-all approach to financial independence; only you will know when you've accomplished it. Be sure to:

- **Reflect on your values and priorities**: Take some time to think about what really matters to you in life. Knowing your core values and priorities is crucial in defining what financial success looks like for you.
- **Envision your ideal future**: Close your eyes and picture yourself 10, 20, or 30 years down the road. Visualizing your ideal future can help you identify the financial milestones that will get you there.
- **Set specific, measurable goals**: Once you have a sense of your values and vision for the future, set your goals. Make sure they are specific, measurable, and achievable so you can track your progress and stay motivated.
- **Consider all aspects of your life**: As you define your version of financial success, consider how it will impact these other areas. Holistic thinking can help you create a definition of success that truly fulfills you.
- **Be flexible and adaptable**: Finally, remember that your definition of financial success is not set in stone. Be open to periodically reassessing it and making adjustments as needed. The key is to stay true to your core values while also being willing to adapt to new circumstances and opportunities.

You can create a roadmap to this financially fulfilling future–one that is uniquely yours!

Aligning Your Values With Your Goals Through Life

What you probably don't know just yet is that your values will change as you grow and mature in life. This means what appeals to you today might not be important to you next year or even next week!

For you to continue aligning your financial goals with the stuff that matters to you in whatever phase of your life you're in, you will need to do some internal work, reflecting on what matters to you at any given moment. To do this, you're going to need to:

- **Consider what is guiding your decisions at the moment**. This could include your family, community, friends, sports, personal growth, etc. Once you know how your values are evolving, you can use them to navigate any financial choices you need to make.
- **Set goals that align with your finances *and* your values.** Setting more goals might sound overwhelming right now, but you will be surprised at how setting life goals and financial goals can show you gaps and patterns in your spending behaviors. When you've identified these gaps, you can better allocate your resources, like your time and money, to the things that matter most to you.
- **Manage your money based on value and values.** If you're using your money to purchase things that align with your values, you're managing your money well. When you buy things based on their value to you, you're managing your money wisely.

Aligning your values with your financial goals might be an ongoing process. Still, by staying true to yourself, you can ensure you have a sound financial roadmap and live a life filled with happiness and purpose.

Common Mistakes You Should Avoid in Pursuing Financial Independence

When you're hot on the heels of your financial independence, there are some things you need to do (the stuff mentioned above) and some things you'll want to avoid to stay on track. These common mistakes can include:

- Not understanding the basics of personal finance
- Not investing in yourself
- Relying on parents for money
- Underestimating the power of saving
- Not keeping track of expenses
- Taking on debt without a repayment plan
- Impulse purchases and fear of missing out (FOMO)
- Not making an effort to increase primary income
- Waiting too long to start saving for retirement

These might seem like a lot of "don'ts", but they shouldn't discourage you. Just stay focused on your goals, surround yourself with people who will support them, and keep on learning and growing. You've got this!

High-Five to Finances: Celebrating Victories On Your Path to Monetary Liberation

Now comes the fun part—what you've been waiting for while working toward your money goals—celebration!

Celebrating your financial wins is more than just a pat on the back, although, if that's what you want to do, more power to you. Finding ways to celebrate the goals you achieve is about building momentum, boosting your motivation, and even inspiring others along the way.

Celebrating your financial victories, no matter how small activates the reward center in your brain—the part that tells you something feels good, and you should make a habit of it. The more you tick off items on your goal list, and the more you celebrate, the more rewards you give your brain and the more likely you are to build a habit out of your financial behaviors.

The more you prove to yourself that you have the ability to create positive change in your life, the more momentum you will build. Think of your financial journey as a rollercoaster—it takes a while to chug on up to the top of the hill but once you get to the pinnacle, it's a wild, smooth sailing ride down to the end.

Added to momentum, celebrating your wins boosts motivation because you've proven repeatedly that you know how to manage your moolah. Setbacks and obstacles become less scary and more like little blips on the map, and you begin to set bigger goals because you no longer fear making a mistake.

Finally, achieving financial success and attaining your goals encourages you to take accountability for your future financial actions. You can look back on the highlight reel of what you've already achieved, using this to inspire you to create and conquer more money goals.

So, remember, celebrating your financial wins is much more than just feeling good. It's about building momentum, boosting your motivation, and creating a ripple of positivity that will be felt right now and in the future. Every win deserves a celebration, every milestone acknowledgment, and every step toward financial independence, a good old hoorah!

Here's an important reminder: celebrating your financial wins doesn't mean going out and blowing your entire savings—that would defeat the object of setting a goal for yourself. You need to know how to celebrate your financial victories in a way that is meaningful to you without splashing all of your hard-earned cash.

- Acknowledge your achievement
- Set and celebrate intermediate goals
- Reward yourself
- Incorporate creativity and fun ideas into your celebration

And remember, celebrating your financial wins is not an optional extra. It's an essential part of your financial success. Make it a priority, get creative with it, and most importantly, have fun with it! Your future self and your bank account will thank you.

Financial Independence Ladder Exercise

Wow, teen, you've reached your final exercise—I hope you're celebrating! In this chapter, you've learned the value and importance of celebrating your financial victories and creating your own definition of financial independence. Now, it is time to put everything together in one place so that you have a celebration checklist.

Step	Milestone Checklist
1. Work on your mindset, uncovering limiting beliefs and turning negative money thoughts into positive ones.	
2. Start generating income, finding possible sources of income, preparing for your interview, and securing your first paycheck.	
3. Put together a budget, working out your expenses and income. Separate this budget into needs, wants, expenses, and savings. Stick to your budget!	
4. Set financial goals for yourself, diving each of your goals into short-, mid-, and long-term. Make sure to use the SMART framework for your financial goals.	
5. Using your budget and your goals, start saving money every month. It doesn't matter if you don't quite reach 20% of your income because every little bit counts.	
6. Manage your debt to build credit. Only spend the money you have, pay off your balances in full when possible, and have a solid plan when lending money for big-ticket purchases.	

7. Invest your saved money to secure your financial future. Set a goal for your investments, assess your risk tolerance, and evaluate your investments often.	
8. Learn to assess, adapt, and change as you encounter challenges or obstacles. Remember that even if something goes wrong, you can adjust your investment portfolio accordingly.	
9. Create your path to financial independence, establishing your definition, aligning your values with your goals, avoiding common mistakes, and celebrating victories.	

And there you have it—all the ultimate money skills you need to achieve financial independence and success! Keep up your financial education, set and smash those goals, and remember you have everything you need to make your money work for you.

PAYING IT FORWARD: EMPOWERING OTHERS

Now that you've equipped yourself with all the tools necessary to master your finances, it's your turn to spread the wealth of knowledge and guide fellow readers to the same enlightenment.

Your journey doesn't end here; it's merely the beginning of a new chapter where you become the mentor, the beacon of guidance for others seeking financial wisdom.

Just as I have shared valuable insights with you, it's time to pay it forward and keep the game of empowerment alive.

Share your experience with others and let them know where they can find the same invaluable resources and support. Together, we can create a ripple effect of financial literacy and empowerment that extends far beyond the confines of these pages.

So, dear reader, as you close this book, remember: your journey towards financial freedom doesn't have to be a solo endeavor. Extend a helping hand, share your knowledge generously, and watch as others follow in your footsteps towards a brighter, more prosperous future.

It's as simple as this: Please leave a review.

Just scan the QR code below to share your thoughts:

Thank you for embarking on this journey with me. Now, go forth and inspire others to do the same.

Your partner in empowerment,

C.K. Roy

CONCLUSION

You are now at the end of this book and well on your way to financial freedom. *The Ultimate Money Skills Handbook for Teens* has provided the tools and knowledge you need to take control of your financial future and create a life of abundance and security. You can decode the language of money, go forward and receive your first paycheck confidently, navigate taxes, create a budget, save, invest, and define wealth for yourself.

But you'll need to remember that financial independence isn't about getting rich quick or having the most expensive things—it's about making smart, intentional choices with your money that align with your values and goals. It's about developing good habits, like budgeting, saving, and investing, and using those habits to build a strong foundation for your future.

So, teen, as you move forward from here, always remember that your definition of financial success is what counts. Surround yourself with positive people who will support your money goals, take proactive steps every day, and sooner than you know it, you'll reap the rewards of your discipline.

You have the power to create a life of financial freedom and abundance, one smart money move at a time. Keep believing in yourself and your dreams, and allow me to say—you've got this!

A Final Request From Me

Creating this book has been a dream of mine for quite some time, so I'd love to hear from you! If you found this book helpful, had something that really resonated with you, or if you've achieved a goal and want to celebrate with like-minded teens, please leave a review. Your feedback and opinion are incredibly valuable to me!

REFERENCES

Arthursson, D. (2016, June 9). *How millennials are defining the sharing economy.* Entrepreneur. https://www.entrepreneur.com/growing-a-business/how-millennials-are-defining-the-sharing-economy/275802

Barrett, B. (2022, May 2). *How to calculate your savings rate and why it's important.* ChooseFI. https://www.choosefi.com/how-to-calculate-your-savings-rate/

Blount, A. (2021, July 29). *Ways to change habits.* Psych Central. https://psychcentral.com/health/steps-to-changing-a-bad-habit

Brown, J., & Wong, J. (2017, June 6). *How gratitude changes you and your brain.* Greater Good; The Greater Good Science Center at the University of California, Berkeley. https://greatergood.berkeley.edu/article/item/how_gratitude_changes_you_and_your_brain

Carolynn Bruce. (2023, August 2). *Average salary by age.* Indeed.com. https://www.indeed.com/career-advice/pay-salary/average-salary-by-age

Chen, O. (2020, December 31). *Maslow's hierarchy of financial needs.* Oz Chen | Financial Educator, Financial Freedom. https://ozchen.com/maslow-hierarchy-needs-money/

Clear, J. (2018, November 13). *The 5 triggers that make new habits stick.* James Clear. https://jamesclear.com/habit-triggers

Dalrymple, R. (2022, August 17). *Wealth hurts your capacity for Empathy: here's what to do about it.* Leaders.com. https://leaders.com/articles/leadership/wealth-hurts-empathy/

Eyring, M., Johnson, M. W., & Nair, H. (2015, May 15). *New business models in emerging markets.* Harvard Business Review. https://hbr.org/2011/01/new-business-models-in-emerging-markets

Ferreri, L., Mas-Herrero, E., Zatorre, R. J., Ripollés, P., Gomez-Andres, A., Alicart, H., Olivé, G., Marco-Pallarés, J., Antonijoan, R. M., Valle, M., Riba, J., & Rodriguez-Fornells, A. (2019). Dopamine modulates the reward experiences elicited by music. *Proceedings of the National Academy of Sciences, 116*(9), 3793–3798. https://doi.org/10.1073/pnas.1811878116

Financial Educators Council. (2023, March 16). *Latest test results indicate American youth fall short in key personal finance knowledge.* Yahoo Finance. https://finance.yahoo.com/news/latest-test-results-indicate-american-123200290.html

Gettysburg College. (2023). *One-third of your life is spent at work.* Gettysburg College. https://www.gettysburg.edu/news/stories?id=79db7b34-630c-4f49-ad32-4ab9ea48e72b#:~

Gold, K. E. (2023, November 8). *You can't earn your way out of stupidity.* Yahoo

Finance.   https://finance.yahoo.com/news/cant-outearn-stupidity-dave-ramsey-110000008.html#:~:

Grewal, D. (2012, April 10). *How wealth reduces compassion?* Scientific American. https://www.scientificamerican.com/article/how-wealth-reduces-compassion/

Hanson, M. (2022, October 24). *Average cost of college [2022]: Yearly tuition + expenses.* Education Data Initiative. https://educationdata.org/average-cost-of-college#:~

Indeed. (2023, December 7). *21 best jobs for teens.* Indeed Career Guide. https://www.indeed.com/career-advice/finding-a-job/best-jobs-for-teens

INTOO. (2019, August 15). *19 fascinating stats on layoff anxiety.* INTOO USA. https://www.intoo.com/us/blog/19-fascinating-stats-on-layoff-anxiety-infographic/

Investor Compound Calculator. (2024). *Compound Interest Calculator | Investor.gov.* Investor.Gov. https://www.investor.gov/financial-tools-calculators/calculators/compound-interest-calculator

Investor.Gov. (2024). *Compound interest Calculator | Investor.gov.* Investor.Gov. https://www.investor.gov/financial-tools-calculators/calculators/compound-interest-calculator

Josephson, A. (2018, June 28). *The average salary by age.* SmartAsset; SmartAsset. https://smartasset.com/retirement/the-average-salary-by-age

Kagan, J. (2022, January 20). *Four Percent Rule.* Investopedia. https://www.investopedia.com/terms/f/four-percent-rule.asp

Kagan, J. (2024, February 4). *Sequence risk: Meaning, retirement, and protection.* Investopedia. https://www.investopedia.com/terms/s/sequence-risk.asp#:~:

Killingsworth, M. A., Kahneman, D., & Mellers, B. (2023). Income and emotional well-being: A conflict resolved. *Proceedings of the National Academy of Sciences, 120*(10). https://doi.org/10.1073/pnas.2208661120

Kumok, Z. (2022, February 6). *How to invest at every age.* Investopedia. https://www.investopedia.com/articles/investing/090915/are-your-investments-right-your-age.asp

Lake, R. (2023, March 3). *Teens and income taxes.* Investopedia. https://www.investopedia.com/teens-and-income-taxes-7152618

Leonard, K. (2020, October 22). *What is a pay stub?* Www.forbes.com. https://www.forbes.com/advisor/business/what-is-pay-stub/

Micalowicz, M. (2013, March 9). *Money amplifies your character.* Mikemichalowicz.com. https://mikemichalowicz.com/money-amplifies-your-character/

Murphy, Chris. B. (2024, February 27). *Debt-to-income (DTI) ratio: What's good and how to calculate it.* Investopedia. https://www.investopedia.com/terms/d/dti.asp#:~

Nerd Wallet. (2024). *Compound interest calculator.* Www.nerdwallet.com. https://www.nerdwallet.com/calculator/compound-interest-calculator

Perkins, B. (2020). *Die with zero: Getting all you can from your money and your life.* Houghton Mifflin Harcourt.

Pfau, W. (2018, January 16). *The Trinity Study and portfolio success rates (Updated To 2018.* Forbes. https://www.forbes.com/sites/wadepfau/2018/01/16/the-trinity-study-and-portfolio-success-rates-updated-to-2018/

Ponzitracker. (2024, January 5). *Ponzitracker.* Ponzitracker. https://www.ponzitracker.com/#:~

Probasco, J. (2024, February 13). *How much do I need to save to retire?* Investopedia. https://www.investopedia.com/retirement/how-much-you-should-have-saved-age/#:~

Robin, V., Dominguez, J. R., & Tilford, M. (2008). *Your money or your life: 9 steps to transforming your relationship with money and achieving financial independence.* Penguin Books.

Rose, S. (2023, September 6). *Ten eye-opening financial literacy statistics.* OppLoans. https://www.opploans.com/oppu/financial-literacy/statistics-financial-literacy/

Rosenfeld, J. (2021, September 29). *Here's how much Americans are spending on coffee.* Yahoo Finance. https://finance.yahoo.com/news/much-americans-spending-coffee-smarter-181719981.html

Royal, J. (2024, March 5). *What is the average stock market return?* NerdWallet. https://www.nerdwallet.com/article/investing/average-stock-market-return#:~

Schwartz, B. (2006, June). *More isn't always better.* Harvard Business Review. https://hbr.org/2006/06/more-isnt-always-better

Stanley, T. J., & Danko, W. D. (2010). *The millionaire next door: The surprising secrets of America's wealthy.* Taylor Trade Publishing.

Statista. (2023). *United States - Monthly inflation rate February 2021/22.* Statista. https://www.statista.com/statistics/273418/unadjusted-monthly-inflation-rate-in-the-us/#:~

Statistica. (2024, February 22). *U.S. average-income teen spending share by category 2018.* Statista. https://www.statista.com/statistics/286937/us-teen-spending-share-by-category/#:~:

Sun, Z., & Xu, X. (2024). Can access to financial markets be an important option for rural families? *Agriculture, 14*(2), 165. https://doi.org/10.3390/agriculture14020165

Susskind, D. (2020). *A world without work: technology, automation, and how we should respond.* Metropolitan Books/Henry Holt And Company.

talent.com. (2024). *Seasonal salary in USA - average salary.* Talent.com. https://www.talent.com/salary?job=Seasonal

The Consumer Bureau of Finance. (2022). *Understanding how much student debt you can afford.* The Consumer Finance Bureau. https://files.consumerfinance.gov/f/

documents/cfpb_building_block_activities_understanding-how-much-student-debt-afford_guide.pdf

The Decision Lab. (2023). *The Paradox of Choice*. The Decision Lab. https://thedecisionlab.com/reference-guide/economics/the-paradox-of-choice

Turner, T. (2023, December 7). *Key financial literacy statistics in 2023*. Annuity.org. https://www.annuity.org/financial-literacy/financial-literacy-statistics/#:~

Voniatis, A. (2023, November 19). *2023 & 2024 ecommerce stats, trends & forecasts*. Artios. https://artios.io/ecommerce-statistics/

Wonderkind. (2024, January 18). *Using social media platforms for recruitment and hiring*. Wonderkind. https://www.wonderkind.com/blog/social-media-platforms-for-recruitment

Made in the USA
Monee, IL
17 October 2024

68162619R00085